EXIT BOMB

Why Most Entrepreneurs Can't Sell, Don't Sell Or Sell Their Companies For Peanuts.

GOWER IDREES

CM&AA, CFP, CEPA

Exit Bomb Organization, LLC
www.ExitBomb.Org
For special discounts for bulk orders, please contact the publisher.

Cover and graphic design by The Business Lab.

ISBN: 978-0692316474

Printed in the United States of America
Published 2015, First Edition
Published simultaneously in electronic format

This book is dedicated to the three pieces of my heart
Luciana, Francesca and Alyson.

And to the enterprising men and women of
Entrepreneurs Organization (EO).

Table of Contents

Part I.
The Exit Bomb

7 Introduction. The Exit Bomb. What It Is and What It Isn't.
10 Chapter 1. Just What the Heck is the Exit Bomb?
20 Chapter 2. Detonator #1: Entrepreneur Factors
37 Chapter 3. Detonator #2: Business Internal Value Destroyers
51 Chapter 4. Detonator #3: Market External Value Impactors
61 Chapter 5. Detonator #4: Buyer Exit Killers, Disruptors and Reducers
79 Chapter 6. Detonator #5: Post-Exit Shockers

Part II.
Defusing the Exit Bomb

100 Chapter 7. Cash is the Problem
103 Chapter 8. Evolving the Entrepreneur Mindset

Value and Risk

107 Chapter 9. Understanding What Creates Value in a Company
112 Chapter 10. Valuation: Entrepreneur vs. Buyer
120 Chapter 11. How Growth Can Hurt Sale Valuation
126 Chapter 12. How Synergies Affect Valuation
132 Chapter 13. Understanding How Risk Affects Value
139 Chapter 14. Understanding the Buyer

Preparing Your Business for Sale

145 Chapter 15. When to Start Getting Ready
148 Chapter 16. Reverse Due Diligence
152 Chapter 17. People Issues
158 Chapter 18. Financial Issues
163 Chapter 19. Sales and Marketing Issues
165 Chapter 20. Operational Issues
168 Chapter 21. Legal Issues
170 Chapter 22. Intellectual Property

173 Chapter 23. Lack of Barriers to Entry

176 Chapter 24. Dealing With Concentrations

179 Chapter 25. The Human Factor

Preparing Yourself for the Exit

184 Chapter 26. Planning Your Exit

188 Chapter 27. Alignment With Your Finances

192 Chapter 28. Timing Your Exit

198 Chapter 29. Net Proceeds: "The Real Wake-Up Call" for Entrepreneurs

202 Chapter 30. Preparing Mentally to Give Up Control

205 Chapter 31. Exit Expertise

The Transaction

210 Chapter 32. Selling the Buyer

215 Chapter 33. Dealing With the Human Obstacles

217 Chapter 34. Letter of Intent

221 Chapter 35. Risk Allocation

225 Chapter 36. Transaction Structure and Taxes

230 Chapter 37. Earn-Outs

234 Chapter 38. Due Diligence: How and Why the Buyer Uses it to Lower Sale Price

241 Chapter 39. The Biggest Deal Killer

244 Chapter 40. Purchase Price Adjustments

251 Chapter 41. Third Parties

253 Chapter 42. Legal Exposures

Conclusion

261 One Last Thing. Or Four.

269 Bibliography

271 Glossary of Terms and Phrases

Part I.
The Exit Bomb

The Exit Bomb®.
What It Is and
What It Isn't.

There are hundreds of books on "how to sell your business." This isn't one of them.

The Exit Bomb is to help keep you from getting screwed when you sell it.

This book is written for entrepreneurs. If you happen to be one, it's for you.

If you're wondering what qualifies me to tell you anything about your business, you should know that I've been an entrepreneur for most of my adult life. Having built and sold a number of businesses, I remain an entrepreneur today as CEO of RareBrain, an M&A firm dedicated to helping entrepreneurial companies grow market share and subsequently sell for maximum value.

Like most entrepreneurs I've met, I've had my share of hard knocks and bloody noses. You might say I've been on easy street and down forty miles of bad roads. In the process, I've learned some things that I want to share with you.

That's why I wrote this book – to keep my fellow entrepreneurs from leaving a pile of money on the table when it comes time to sell the companies they've built.

I've seen far too many business owners trade the results of a lifetime of hard work for a payout of peanuts. I've seen retirement plans dashed and owners working way into their seventies. I've seen the faces of still others when they discover their company simply can't be sold.

I've dealt with hundreds of entrepreneurs. I've also met countless more as a former member of EO, the Entrepreneurs Organization, and have traveled around the world attending conferences of entrepreneurs.

Several years ago, I set out to uncover how to stop the entrepreneur's business wealth from virtually evaporating when he or she exits the business. Since I already had context from my own business exits and from being involved in two decades of financial transactions, I studied the missing elements in order to create a comprehensive and structured program to help entrepreneurs maximize value in a business exit.

After years of hard work, I've created a number of specialized tools, exit programs and workshops to help entrepreneurs and the independent advisors who work with them prevent value destruction when exiting a business.

To make all this available to the greatest number of entrepreneurs possible, I decided to launch a privately held organization designed to help them clean up, enhance value and exit their companies on their own terms and time line . . . and for maximum value. It's the Exit Bomb Organization™. (To learn more, visit www.ExitBomb.Org.)

If I put everything you need to know about exiting a business into one book, you probably wouldn't be able to lift it. So what I'm going to do in this one is share the key concepts, strategies and tactics that are used in the Exit Bomb Organization's "Exit Maximization Programs." (You can see some of these at www.ExitBomb.Org/Programs.)

The Exit Bomb book is the first step and a critical one. It's a road map to helping you understand what can destroy your business value and how to avoid that kind of destruction – which makes this book one of the best investments you could make in your business.

But maybe you're not worried about "Exit Bombs" and "wealth destruction." That's understandable.

One of the problems with us entrepreneurs is that we read about marquee acquisitions and big exits in newspapers and social media. Our reaction is, "Wow! That guy sold for $200 million." This can motivate us, inspire us and, in many cases, make us believe we can do the same.

Or one of our golfing buddies tells us that a neighbor sold his or her company for 17X.

This sets our expectations that our companies are worth as much. In M&A speak, we call those "country club multiples."

What we don't hear about are the bulk of other private transactions that had horrid valuations or were drastically discounted due to all kinds of issues. Nobody talks about them. They simply aren't sexy.

There is nothing wrong with dreaming big. My advice is to not get caught up in those "dream deals." While you're dreaming big, you also need to stay real and remember this: Eight out of ten businesses don't sell. Not at any price.

Substantially increasing the value of your company so it can sell – and sell for maximum value – requires a focused effort. Considering that it's the result of your life's work we're talking about, it's well worth the effort.

If you'll stay with me, I will take you on a knowledge journey that can lead to a successful exit and all the rewards that come with it.

Ready?

Chapter 1.

Just What the Heck is an Exit Bomb?

Almost every business has one. Yours probably does, too.

In fact, I'd be willing to bet on it.

You can't hear this bomb ticking. Even if you did, you've been so busy building your business you probably wouldn't have noticed anyway.

This bomb is attached to that door marked "EXIT." Open the door and …

BOOM!

Your hard-earned wealth gets blown to bits.

The Exit Bomb keeps 80% of businesses listed for sale from selling.[1] And prevents 70% of all family businesses from being passed on to the kids.[2]

So what is this Bomb? It's that nasty surprise that awaits far too many entrepreneurs when the time comes to "exit" their companies.

The Exit Bomb is the reason so many leave a big chunk of their life's work on the table when they sell. And the main contributor to wrecked retirements and seller's remorse.

1 Small Business Administration (SBA)
2 Family Firm Institute

It's why you see seventy-year-olds selling suits at Brooks Brothers instead of sitting on a beach somewhere with one of those umbrella drinks in their hands. The reason so many family businesses aren't in the family any more. And the cause of plenty of entrepreneurs ending up with little to show for a lifetime of effort.

For a great many entrepreneurs, there are only two outcomes from an Exit Bomb explosion.

A Failed Exit. The business doesn't sell. Which means anguish, frustration and that sense of being trapped.

A Completed Exit. But one with a lot of post-exit "gotchas." Which translates into anguish, frustration and seller's remorse.

The Exit Bomb has five highly explosive elements. I call these "detonators."

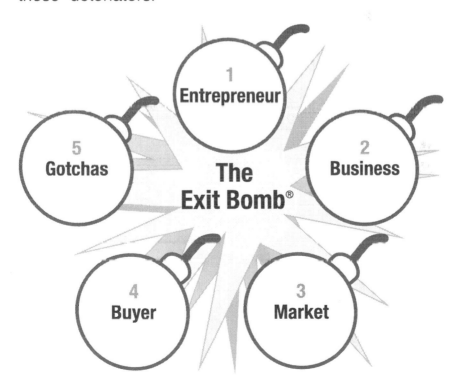

Any one of these five detonators can go off by itself. Which results in significant destruction to the business's value.

Or, worse, they can all fire at once. And that causes truly catastrophic destruction of the value of the business.

Here's a preview of each one.

Detonator #1. Entrepreneur Factors. This is where, as entrepreneurs, our personality and psychological factors – plus our knowledge gaps – help destroy the value of the business.

Detonator #2. Business Internal Value Destroyers. These are inefficiencies and deficiencies within the business that decrease its value.

Detonator #3. Market External Value Impactors. These are external factors such as the state of the economy that can lower business value.

Detonator #4. Buyer Exit Killers, Disruptors and Reducers. These involve buyer factors such as adverse findings, price revisions etc.

Detonator #5. Post-Exit Shockers. These are all the "gotchas" that many entrepreneurs experience after the sale. Tax surprises and financial shortfalls are just two of them.

Let's take a quick look at each of these detonators.

Detonator #1.
Entrepreneur Factors

We entrepreneurs have unique strengths that make us … well … entrepreneurs.

Problem is these strengths often turn into weaknesses when we sell the business.

These weaknesses, combined with some other elements, I call the "Entrepreneur Factors."

These factors are often directly responsible for value destruction.

In other words, Detonator #1.

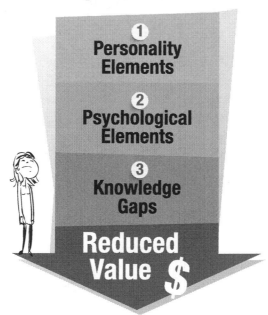

Entrepreneur Factors

1. Personality Elements
2. Psychological Elements
3. Knowledge Gaps

Reduced Value $

Detonator # 2.
Business Internal Value Destroyers

There's no "Entrepreneur U." No school that teaches us how to be entrepreneurs.

So we make it up as we go along. That usually works okay except that along the way, we build in all kinds of inefficiencies in the business.

These inefficiencies can destroy the value of your business and you won't know it until it comes time to sell.

That's why I call them "Business Internal Value Destroyers."

You can call them Detonator #2.

Detonator #3:
Market External Value Impactors

Are you ready for the biggest business sell-off in history?

It's coming. And so are a lot of other external factors that can severely cripple your business – and its valuation at exit time.

I call these factors "Market Business External Value Impactors." Here are some of the triggers that could lead to detonation.

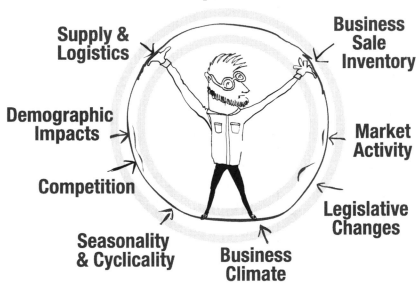

Market External Value Impactors

- Supply & Logistics
- Business Sale Inventory
- Demographic Impacts
- Market Activity
- Competition
- Legislative Changes
- Seasonality & Cyclicality
- Business Climate

Detonator #4.
Buyer Exit Killers, Disruptors and Reducers

You'll probably sell a business once in your lifetime. The typical buyer is in the market for businesses often.

Who do you think will come out ahead at sale time?

Here are some of the things that can be called "Buyer Exit Killers, Disruptors and Reducers."

Or, more simply, Detonator #4.

Competencies
Deficiencies
Tactics
Disputes
Egos

Valuation/Price
Consideration
Taxes

Deal Structure
Terms & Conditions
Risk Allocations

Financing
3rd Parties
Lawsuits

Adverse Findings
Price Revisions

Deal Fatigue
Deal Remorse
Momentum Loss

Detonator #5.
Post-Exit Shockers

You're sitting on a beach having a drink with an umbrella in it. You've earned it.

You went through all the pain and misery of selling your business. But now it's sold and you can relax.

Then your phone rings and it's the buyer telling you the purchase price has been reduced by a million bucks. That check that was in the mail? It isn't.

That's just one of what I call the "Post-Exit Shockers." They're Detonator #5.

I Got Screwed!
Purchase Price Adjustments

Working Capital Adjustments

Earn-Out Fizzle

They Want My Savings!
Legal Exposure

Financial Exposure

What the Heck?!
Seller's Remorse

Loss of Identity

Family Conflicts

Post-Exit Shockers

No One Told Me!
Net Proceeds Gotcha

Tax Surprises

Headaches!
Payment Defaults

Excluded Obligations

Liquidity

I HATE This!
Employment

No Compete

No Control

The plain truth is that most entrepreneurs aren't ready to sell their businesses even if they had to do it today. Most don't have businesses that are even close to being ready to be sold or transferred.

That's the Exit Bomb, my friend.

It's something almost every entrepreneur will have to deal with. Because the harsh reality is that all of us must leave our businesses one day either voluntarily or not.

So think hard and ask yourself this question:

Am I building a business to sell or to shut down?

While you ponder that, let's take a longer look at these detonators I told you about.

Detonator

#1

Entrepreneur Factors

Entrepreneurs are great at generating cash.
But we're even better at destroying value.

Chapter 2.

Entrepreneur Factors

Can you handle some cold, hard truth?

Okay, here it comes.

The qualities that make entrepreneurs successful are the same ones that can reduce the value of the business when it comes time to sell.

That's BS, you say. Completely crazy. Just nuts.

Well, before you stop reading, let me explain.

As I told you, I'm an entrepreneur and I've got the scars to prove it. Along the way, I've learned a few things.

What I learned was that there are three elements that are the core of why we don't maximize exit value. They are:

1. **Personality Elements.** Personality traits, qualities and strengths.

2. **Psychological Elements.** Exit motivations and influencers.

3. **Knowledge Gaps.** Exit-related knowledge and expertise gaps.

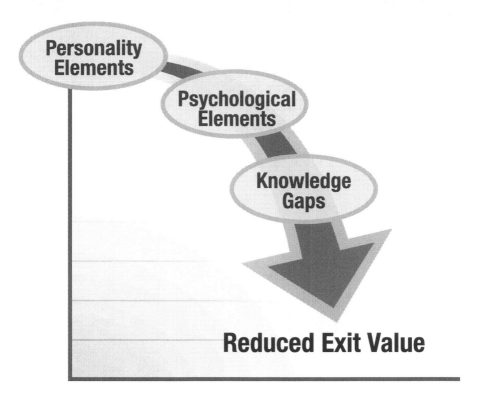

What I also learned was that I had to overcome something else. They were my own …

Personality Elements

In other words, I had to learn to control the very strengths – the elements of my personality – that led to my success as an entrepreneur in order to master the art of selling a business.

Was it tough? You bet. But I did it and so can you.

Still not convinced you need to do all that? Let's look at some of the ways our personality elements – the traits that make us successful entrepreneurs – get in the way of a successful sale.

Entrepreneur personality element:
We're risk takers.

Entrepreneur mindset:
We're willing to bet the farm to get our business where we want it to go.

How this can hurt exit value:
Because we're so used to taking risks in our business, we have no idea how a buyer might view risk.

Example:
When we drive a car fast, we might feel in control but the passengers don't. Their experience is entirely different. It's the same with an entrepreneur and a buyer.

Entrepreneur personality element:
We have to be in control.

Entrepreneur mindset:
We must be involved in all the details. Nothing important can happen without us.

How this can hurt exit value:
Our business relies so heavily on us that it doesn't seem likely to survive without us.

Example:
Imagine leaving your business for a year. Would your business still be standing when you got back? Now, imagine leaving permanently. If you're not around, chances are the business won't be either. Can you blame a potential buyer for heading for the door?

Entrepreneur personality element:
We have authority issues. And we have problems with somebody else's rules.

Entrepreneur mindset:
We're the boss. Can't be any other way.

How this can hurt exit value:
We don't make the best employees.

Example:
Even if the deal calls for us to stick around after the sale, we often can't. We either get fired or quit. Either way, we leave a pile of money on the table.

Entrepreneur personality element:
We're crazy for cash flow.

Entrepreneur mindset:
Any day with positive cash flow
is a good day.

How this can hurt exit value:
Our focus on cash-flow generation
keeps us from doing things that
would build the value of the business
and sustain it long term. And that
reduces the company's value at
selling time.

Example:
Remind me to tell you about the
entrepreneur with a $5 million
revenue business. It survived six
months after he died.

Entrepreneur personality element:
We're too damned optimistic.

Entrepreneur mindset:
Things are bound to get better.
Something will turn up.

How this can hurt exit value:
We don't plan. Who's got time
for that?

Example:
According to a recent survey,
three out of four business
owners say they have not done
any exit planning.

Entrepreneur personality element:
We get bored easily.
And we're impatient.

Entrepreneur mindset:
Spare me the details and
cut to the chase.

How this can hurt exit value:
Implementing initiatives to increase
the value of the company requires
tremendous focus and commitment.
That's not us. We don't stay engaged
and our impatience keeps us from
following through.

Example:
Do you find yourself tuning out at
meetings? Does your patience wear
thin if you don't see results right
away? Are you tempted to skip to the
last chapter of this book?

Entrepreneur personality element:
We have rather large egos.

Entrepreneur mindset:
Our business and our products are extensions of ourselves. If we don't believe in our company, products and ourselves, how can we expect others to?

How this can hurt exit value:
We have difficulty accepting critiques from prospective buyers.

Example:
When a would-be buyer brings up a negative, we get defensive and that sometimes ends negotiations.

Entrepreneur personality element:

We frequently sacrifice personal needs over those of the business.

Entrepreneur mindset:

The business comes first. We're willing to sacrifice in hopes of a big payoff sometime in the future.

How this can hurt exit value:

We create an unrealistic sale price because we figure somebody has to pay for all our hard work, forgetting that personal sacrifice never shows up on the balance sheet.

Example:

It's like loving your house so much that you list it for far more than any other house in the neighborhood. And then you see it sit unsold for months until you finally bring the price down to what it's really worth.

Don't get me wrong. I'm not saying you have to change your entire personality and go from Jekyll to Hyde.

What I'm telling you is that you need to recognize those entrepreneur-oriented personality elements and control them in order to sell your company for the biggest payout possible.

Trust me, it'll be worth it.

Now, if your personality elements weren't enough to get in the way of a successful sale, the very things that are motivating you to sell can work against you. These are …

Psychological Elements

They fall into a couple of categories: Exit Motivations and Exit Influencers. Let's take the first one first.

Exit Motivations

There are plenty of reasons you might want to exit your business. But whatever your reason, you're doing one of two things.

You're either sprinting away from your business or sprinting toward the next chapter in your life. Here are some of the reasons you might be sprinting away:

Sprinting away from their existing business

< LOWER VALUE

Changing Market Landscape
Growth & Operating Capital Needs
Obsolescence
Skill Gaps
Business Problems
Boredom
Burnout
Lack of Successors

Business Owner

And here's what sprinting toward the next chapter looks like:

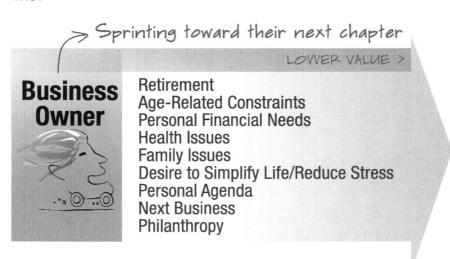

Sprinting toward their next chapter

LOWER VALUE >

Business Owner

Retirement
Age-Related Constraints
Personal Financial Needs
Health Issues
Family Issues
Desire to Simplify Life/Reduce Stress
Personal Agenda
Next Business
Philanthropy

What you need to know about both is this:

EXIT MOTIVATION = LIKELY VALUE REDUCTION

Why?

Because by the time you are motivated to exit, it may be too late to get the maximum value from your company.

You see, enhancing the value of your company takes time, energy and financial resources. And by the time you're ready to exit, you're in the last lap of the race.

You don't have that time, that energy or the desire to invest in value enhancement.

Your foot is already off the gas.

There's another reason why motivation can lead to value reduction. Buyers are great at sniffing out exit motivations and they're ready to take full advantage of the situation.

After all, wouldn't you?

Exit Decision Influencers

Besides those exit motivations, you've got other influencers that can disrupt or reduce value in the sale of your business. They often wreak havoc on the decision making process.

Exit decision influencers come in all shapes and sizes. Some of them are personal biases and agendas. The thing to remember is that when those biases rule the day the exit options can be limited. So can the selling price.

For example, would you refuse to sell to a competitor just because you lost a big deal to them last year ... even if they would offer the biggest payout? Or would you turn down an offer from a company whose religious beliefs you didn't share?

It is, of course, your prerogative to sell to whomever you want. But it's important to understand which exit influencer is a strategic business decision and which one limits your selling options and, very likely, your selling price.

Exit Bomb. Why Most Entrepreneurs Can't Sell, Don't Sell or Sell Their Company For Peanuts.

Exit Knowledge Gaps

Sure, you're the expert when it comes to your company. You know your business better than anybody else. And you know how to run it.

But running a company and selling it are two very different things.

Which means there are probably things you don't know about selling a business that will reduce its value and the money you get from its sale. It may even derail the sale.

These knowledge gaps fall into six areas:

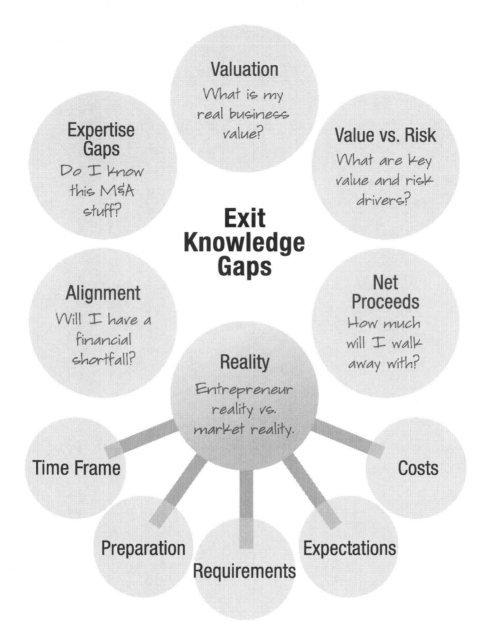

Exit Knowledge Gaps

Valuation — What is my real business value?

Value vs. Risk — What are key value and risk drivers?

Expertise Gaps — Do I know this M&A stuff?

Net Proceeds — How much will I walk away with?

Alignment — Will I have a financial shortfall?

Reality — Entrepreneur reality vs. market reality.

Time Frame

Costs

Preparation

Requirements

Expectations

Wow! That's a lot of gaps. Don't worry. By the time we're through, you'll have a fair idea of how to bridge them.

Besides, that's just the first detonator. There are more to come. Brace yourself.

Detonator
#2
Business
Internal Value
Destroyers

We entrepreneurs get so good at putting out fires we become great firefighters.

What we don't realize is that we're actually the arsonists.

Chapter 3.

Business Internal Value Destroyers

Nothing really prepares us to be entrepreneurs. It's not something you can learn in school. There are no manuals because every business is different. And we wouldn't take time to read them even if there were.

Most of us make it up as we go along. As a result, we build in a lot of inefficiencies.

Unfortunately, these inefficiencies can dramatically reduce the value of our companies when we decide to sell.

I call them …

"Business Internal Value Destroyers."

Sure, we could fix most of them if we had the time to focus and do some planning. But with all the demands and pressure on us just to keep our businesses alive, we never take the time.

Then one morning we wake up and decide it's time to sell. Maybe we're just tired or we read about some new technology that could hurt our business. Or maybe we figure it's time to retire or we've got health or family issues.

The shock comes when we discover that either our business can't be sold. Or if somebody does want to buy it, the price doesn't even come close to what you had in mind.

And it's all because those problems never got fixed.

That's what is known as Detonator #2.

So what are these Business Internal Value Destroyers? Here are a few:

Let's take a closer look at some of them.

Lack of Planning

Planning! Who's got the time for that? But without planning, the business won't reach its full potential. And the buyer won't have a clear road map of how the company will sustain revenues, margins and profits. Which, of course, means it's worth less to the potential buyer.

Here are a few of the things that should be in place:

People Issues

Your employees just might be your most important asset. But they can also be your biggest problem. Because without safeguards in place to keep key employees around after you sell, they may not be there for the next owner. On the other hand, costly employment agreements and high labor costs can be twin turn-offs for the buyer.

So can lack of depth in the management team. See what I mean about people issues?

Like these:

Financial Issues

Would you buy a house if you couldn't verify how many square feet it contained? Or if the seller refused to allow you to have it inspected? Nobody will want to buy a business if your financials aren't totally transparent. If the buyer doesn't trust them, they'll offer a low-ball price to counter their risk or they'll take a pass. Lack of financial transparency will mean you'll likely never see a check for your asking price.

Here are some examples of financial issues:

Sales and Marketing Issues

The lack of an effective marketing strategy means your company suffers from low market share, minimal visibility and, of course, poor sales. All of which makes a company less than desirable from a buyer's point of view. Sure, he could come in with a bold new strategy and do some real marketing. But why should he pay you a premium for the business when he's got to spend his money to make it fully functional?

These are some sales and marketing issues buyers will spot:

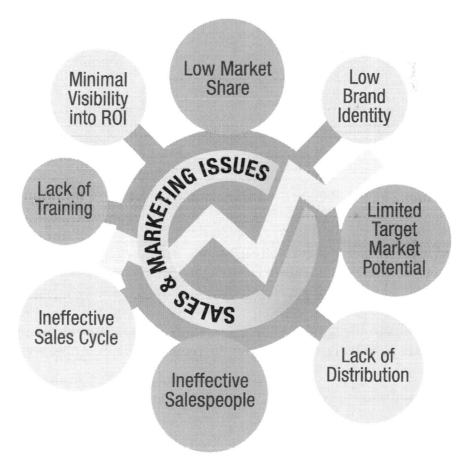

Financial Performance

Of course you want to see your company make money. That's what buyers are looking for, too. They want to see a positive revenue trend line. Inconsistent revenues and margin trends … not so much. Neither do they want to find flat revenue growth or declining order backlogs. Any of these could be signs of ineffective management or something deeply wrong with the company. Either one could spell no sale or a sale at a vastly reduced price.

A few typical financial performance problems:

Current Position Weaknesses

Buyers buy momentum. They want to make sure they can get their investment back plus a handsome return on it in a reasonable period of time. If your company's current position is weak in any of a number of areas, its value is reduced and so is the sale price. That is, if the would-be buyer isn't motivated to simply walk away.

Some possible weaknesses:

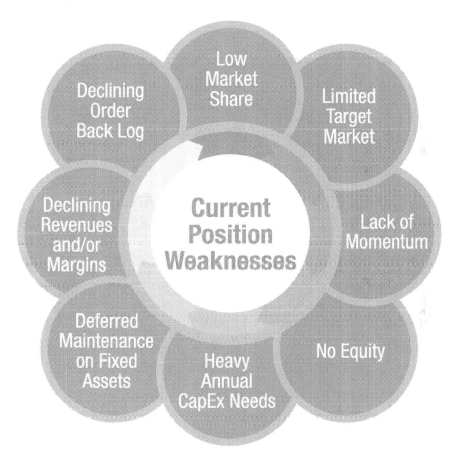

Products and Services

Simply put, the easier your products and services are to replicate, the less likely you'll be paid top dollar for your business. The lack of barriers-to-entry for a potential rival can reduce the exit value of your company considerably. Low margins and outdated business models don't help either.

Some typical problems in this area:

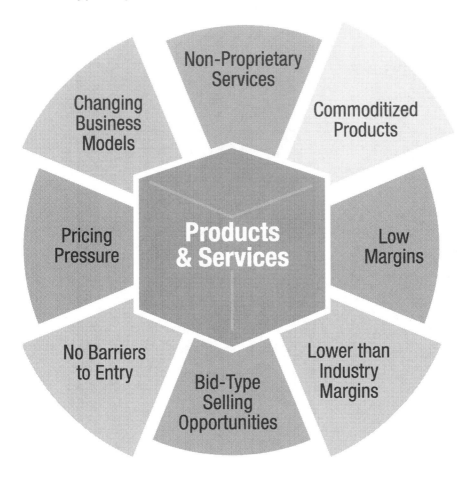

Operational Issues

Lack of operational controls hurts productivity, margins and momentum. Which in turn sucks up cash and lowers profits. And while a potential buyer may assume less than effective management on your part, he might also become concerned that there are deeper issues involved. Care to guess what all that does to your exit valuation?

A few typical operational issues:

Buyer Risks

Buyers are looking for growth potential at minimal risk. And, naturally, risk is the last thing on an entrepreneur's mind. As a result, our companies are often chock-full of all kinds of buyer risk. Any one of those could be a value killer. Or likely a deal killer.

Some common buyer risks:

Intellectual Property

Let's face it. We entrepreneurs don't focus enough on our intellectual property assets – even though they can be a big chunk of our company's valuation. Often we don't understand that our intellectual property is a hedge against risk and can protect revenue. Many of us have no cohesive strategy for collecting, documenting and protecting these assets. As a result, they aren't properly considered in determining the company's valuation. And that means a major reduction in value.

Some frequent intellectual property issues:

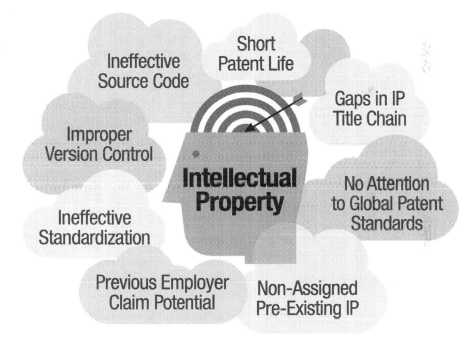

Pretty scary, huh?

Yeah, but there's hope. That is, if you take the time to fix those value destroyers now … before you start thinking about selling your company.

Stay with me and I'll show you how to turn those value destroyers into value drivers. Those drivers will increase your company's value. And the size of the check you'll walk away with.

Detonator
#3
*Market
External Value
Impactors*

You may not be able to control them.
But you don't have to be blindsided.

Chapter 4.

Market External Value Impactors

You're taking care of business … doing all the right things for your company … looking ahead and planning.

Then BANG! Something that's totally out of your control puts a major hurt on your business. Maybe it's a bunch of new regulations that changes your cost economies. Or perhaps one of your competitors introduces a new product that will make yours obsolete.

I call these factors "Market External Value Impactors." And while they might not actually kill your company, any one of them can wound it severely.

Here are a few of them:

Market External Value Impactors

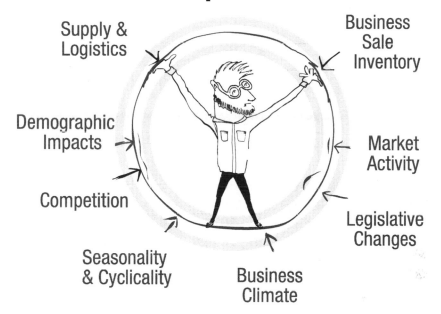

Supply & Logistics

Business Sale Inventory

Demographic Impacts

Market Activity

Competition

Seasonality & Cyclicality

Business Climate

Legislative Changes

The Coming Baby Boomer Business Sell-Off

Baby Boomers own more than 50% of all private businesses in the United States.

So what?

Here's what … seventy-five percent of them plan to exit their businesses over the next ten years.

That's the biggest business sell-off in history.

This massive sell-off means a transfer of 4.5 million businesses and over ten trillion dollars in wealth.

Just guess what that is going to do to the market.

And imagine what it will do to your sale price if you decide to sell your business anytime during the next five to ten years.

Market Activity

I'm not talking about the Dow or the NASDAQ, here. I'm talking about activity in the real marketplace that can affect the value of your company now and when you sell it.

Not all of this activity is necessarily negative. But even positive changes can disrupt markets and have an impact on your business.

It's smart to keep an eye out for such activity as a wave of consolidations and regulatory changes so you can take steps to help your business weather them.

Here are a few examples:

Business Climate

Of course, the overall business climate is going to have an impact on the sale of your business. If the cost of capital is high, that's going to drive down the price.

And if the business environment is unsettled, you may have trouble finding a buyer.

Even if the sale is some distance in the future, a negative business climate may affect the day-to-day operation of your company and may keep you from implementing some of the improvements that will increase its value.

Some factors that impact the business climate:

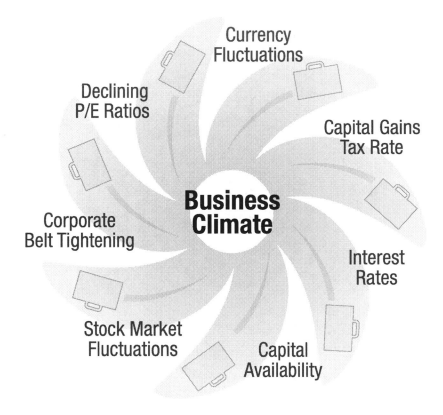

Currency Fluctuations

Declining P/E Ratios

Capital Gains Tax Rate

Business Climate

Corporate Belt Tightening

Interest Rates

Stock Market Fluctuations

Capital Availability

Competition

You know your competitors are out to eat your lunch. Competition from them can also eat into the valuation of your company at exit time.

Maybe they're into aggressive pricing in order to grab market share. Maybe they've introduced a product that puts yours in the shade. Or maybe they've got a built-in competitive advantage such as manufacturing their products in a low-wage country.

In any case, you've got to keep an eye on – and be one step ahead of – your competition if you don't plan on leaving the table hungry.

Here's how your competition can impact you:

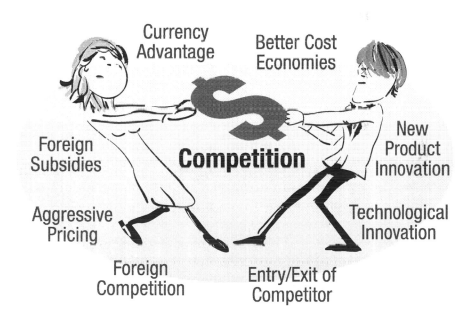

Demographic and Social Changes

What's relevant today may not be relevant tomorrow. Consumer tastes and behavior won't stay static. Cultural shifts and attitudes change.

While you can't control these changes, you can be aware of them. In fact, you must be if you don't want to be left behind.

You may not be the first to spot a trend. But you certainly don't want to be the last to see it.

Here are some of these consumer aspects to watch out for:

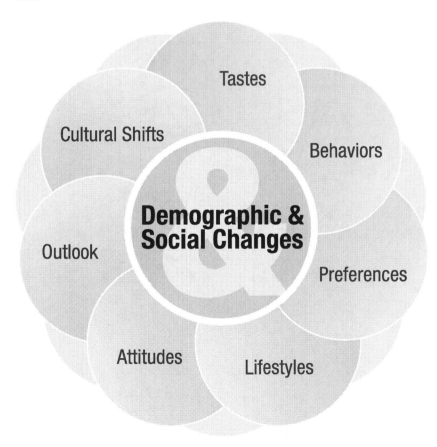

Supply and Logistics

Changes in supply-chain costs, efficiencies and availability can impact exit valuation. Suppose your product is being made in China and the price of raw materials goes up by 25%.

Now imagine you're at the closing table when this happens. Do you think it just might have an impact on your sale price?

Here are some of the ways that changes in supply and logistics can impact the sale price of your company:

So what's an entrepreneur to do?

Even though a lot of these factors are beyond your control, you don't have to sit there and wait for the roof to fall in.

Detonator

#4

Buyer Exit Killers, Disruptors and Reducers

You probably know the phrase "Caveat Emptor," which means "Let the buyer beware."

What about the seller?

Chapter 5.

Buyer Exit Killers, Disruptors and Reducers

Look at it this way. The typical entrepreneur sells a business once in a lifetime. The typical buyer buys businesses all the time. For some, buying businesses is their business.

Who do you think is going to come out ahead?

If you want it to be you, you might want to pay particular attention to this chapter. It's all about Detonator #4 – Buyer Exit Killers, Disruptors and Reducers.

- Valuation/Price
- Consideration
- Taxes

- Deal Structure
- Terms & Conditions
- Risk Allocation

- Competencies
- Deficiencies
- Tactics
- Disputes
- Egos

MONEY

DEAL

Buyer Exit Killers, Disruptors & Reducers

HUMANS

TIME

EXTERNAL

SCRUTINY

- Deal Fatigue
- Deal Remorse
- Momentum Loss

- Financing
- 3rd Parties
- Lawsuits

- Adverse Findings
- Price Revisions

Valuation and Price

The entrepreneur and the potential buyer see these quite differently. And that can cause the deal to fall apart.

The Buyer's View of Value

Book Value
Asset Value
Market Value
Fair Market Value
Investment Value
Synergized Value
Public Market Value

The Entrepreneur's View of Value

Sacrifice Value

Lifestyle/Income
Replacement Value

Opportunity Value

Unrealistic Value

Rumor Value

Consideration

Most entrepreneurs focus on price when selling their businesses. What they should be focused on is the total consideration being offered.

By "total consideration," I mean the total amount of money being offered plus all kinds of caveats. These caveats can mean plenty of "gotchas" which means you'll never see your full selling price unless you know what to watch out for.

Consideration can take many forms:

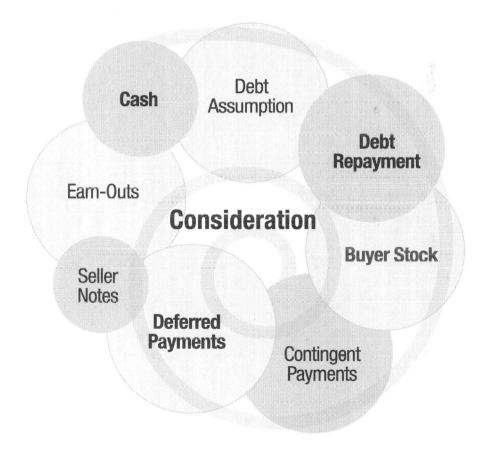

Deal Structure and Taxes

These can make or break a transaction. Or, at the very least, leave you with a lot less money than you thought you were going to have.

Many entrepreneurs find out about the tax consequences of the deal after they've signed a binding purchase and sale agreement. It's too late then for anything but tears.

Most entrepreneurs pay far too much in taxes. Tax impact can range from 20% to 60%+ in federal and state taxes depending on the type of entity being sold, the transaction structure and where you live.

That's the result of waiting until closing to do tax planning.

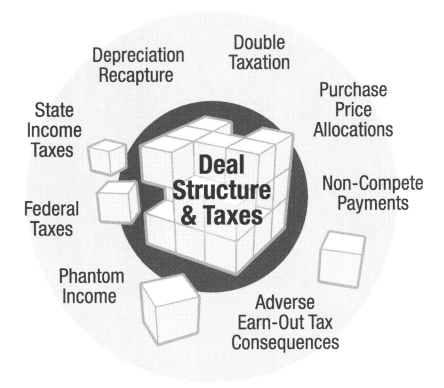

Risk Allocation

When most entrepreneurs are selling a business, they're thinking about maximizing the selling price.

The buyer, on the other hand, is thinking about how he can minimize his purchase price – the price he'll have to pay.

But that's not all. The buyer is also thinking of ways to keep the poor entrepreneur on the hook in case some hidden liabilities come to light or if the seller has misrepresented something.

Basically, the buyer is trying to shift risk to the entrepreneur. Here are some of the ways he or she may try to do that:

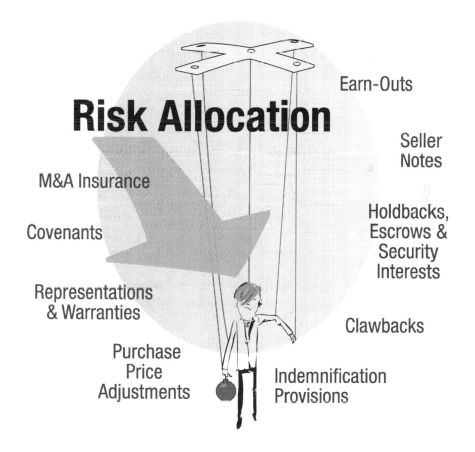

Terms and Conditions

Sure, there have to be some sort of terms and conditions for the sale of your business.

Problem is these are usually drawn up by the buyer's lawyer. They're designed to minimize risk for his client. And that means they're almost always weighted in the buyer's favor.

Here are some of them:

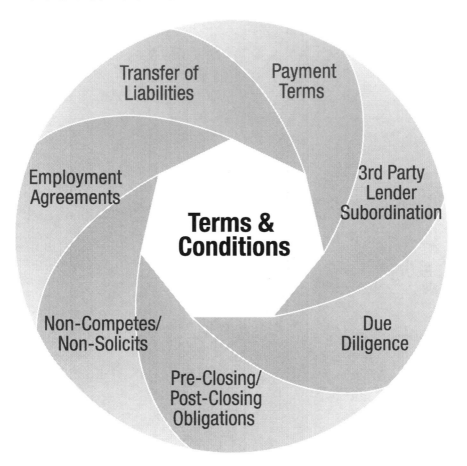

Time

It is the #1 killer of deals and it definitely isn't on your side. The sales transaction may drag on for so long that both the buyer and the entrepreneur get what's called "transaction fatigue."

So the deal often ends up not getting done because the buyer has had too much time to think the whole thing over and decides against it. Or the entrepreneur comes down with a case of "deal remorse."

Either way, the sale goes south even though both parties have invested a tremendous amount of effort, resources and … yes … time into it.

Time can create transaction remorse for both the seller and the buyer. Here are a few examples of each:

Changing Market Conditions

Emotional Toll

Transaction Fatigue

Seller Deal Remorse

New Contracts/ Opportunities

Increasing Revenues & Cash Flow

Due Diligence

Most entrepreneurs are not prepared for the level of scrutiny, the lengthy time frame, the associated costs and the distraction to his or her business that come with due diligence.

Here are a few of the things entrepreneurs underestimate:

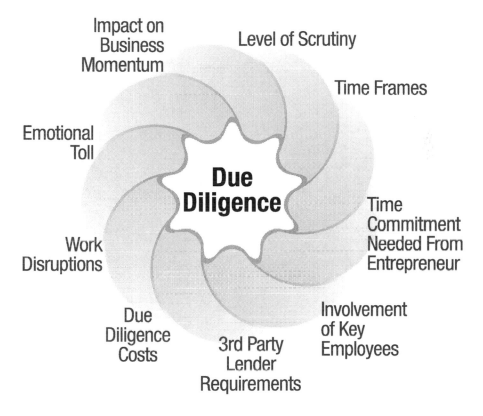

Impact on Business Momentum

Level of Scrutiny

Time Frames

Emotional Toll

Due Diligence

Time Commitment Needed From Entrepreneur

Work Disruptions

Due Diligence Costs

3rd Party Lender Requirements

Involvement of Key Employees

Due Diligence Surprises

Many deals die a dozen deaths during due diligence. The process can stretch on for months and all sorts of things can surface. These can either hurt the selling price or increase the cost of due diligence for everybody. No wonder it's such a dangerous period.

Here are just a few due diligence surprises:

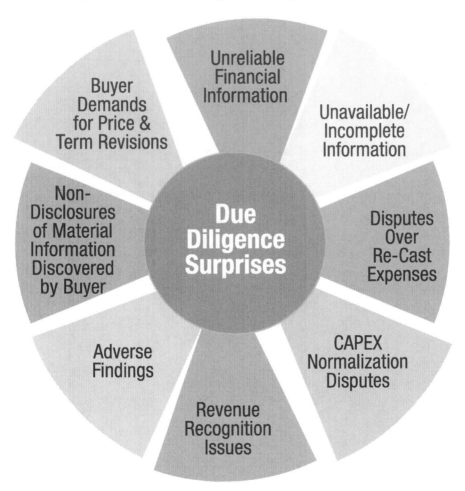

Third-Party Financing

It would never occur to most entrepreneurs to actually make it easier for the buyer to obtain third-party financing. Entrepreneurs almost never consider their role in helping facilitate lender-driven due diligence. Instead, the entrepreneur can get in the way of the sale and raise the stress and complexity level of the deal.

Here are some of the hurdles involved in third-party financing:

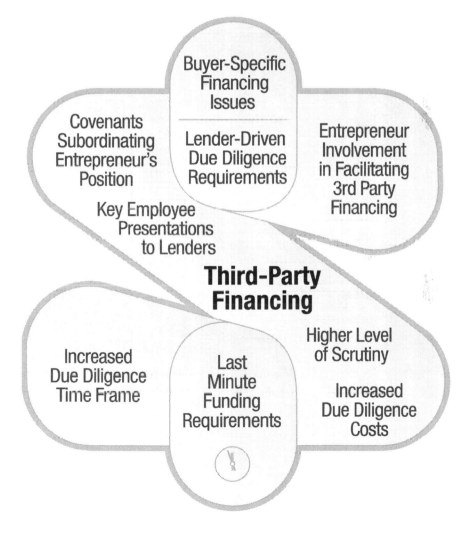

Buyer-Specific Financing Issues

Covenants Subordinating Entrepreneur's Position

Lender-Driven Due Diligence Requirements

Entrepreneur Involvement in Facilitating 3rd Party Financing

Key Employee Presentations to Lenders

Third-Party Financing

Increased Due Diligence Time Frame

Last Minute Funding Requirements

Higher Level of Scrutiny

Increased Due Diligence Costs

Third Parties

Speaking of which, they can play a huge role in whether the transaction gets done or not. Even when the buyer and seller have an agreement and everybody's happy, along comes a third party to kill the deal. Since the entrepreneur isn't in the habit of thinking about third parties in running the business, he or she doesn't think about them when selling.

And the entrepreneur gets blindsided.

Here are some of the third parties who can kill the deal:

Lawsuits, Claims and Disputes

Exits often get derailed because of a lawsuit or even the threat of one. Many times, disputes can have material repercussions on the future of the business.

Here are some examples of what can derail an exit:

The Human Factor

Humans are behind the creation of wealth. They're also responsible for its destruction when it comes to selling the business. When otherwise rational buyers and sellers and their advisors become so protective of their respective turf, all kinds of disputes result. Those lead to tremendous transactional stress and, sometimes, the death of the deal.

Here are some examples of human behavior that can wreck an exit:

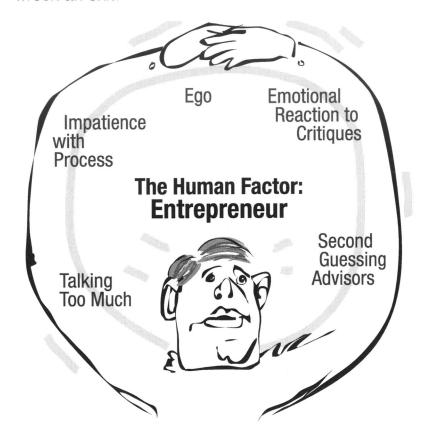

Ego

Emotional Reaction to Critiques

Impatience with Process

The Human Factor: Entrepreneur

Second Guessing Advisors

Talking Too Much

Advisors

The Human Factor:
Advisors

Ego Clashes

Limited Understanding of M&A Process

Slow Turnaround Times

Getting Bogged Down in Minutiae

Failing to Filter Information to Protect Client

Inexperienced Players (Buy-Side/Sell-Side)

Shareholders & Stakeholders

The Human Factor:
Shareholders

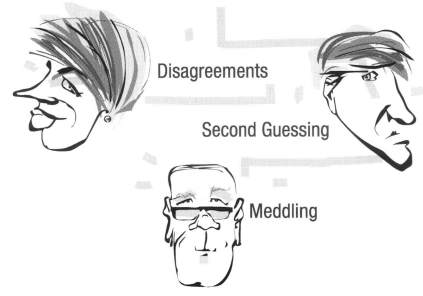

Disagreements

Second Guessing

Meddling

Detonator #5: Post-Exit Shockers

Three out of four entrepreneurs suffer seller's remorse within twelve months of selling their businesses.[3]

Will you?

3 Exit Planning Institute - PricewaterhouseCoopers survey of former business owners

Chapter 6.

Post-Exit Shockers

I have yet to meet an entrepreneur who has sold his or her business that did not have some after-the-sale "gotcha" story.

By "gotcha" I mean some unexpected ploy that the buyer used after the closing to reduce the sale price or otherwise make the seller sorry he or she sold in the first place.

Since the entrepreneur seldom sees these coming, they come as a shock. That's why I call them "Post-Exit Shockers."

These shockers result from a number of things. Among them, the entrepreneur's lack of preparation, lack of knowledge and not fully understanding the implications and legal consequences of various structures and tactics.

To my mind, this is the worst detonator of all. You might think that a failed exit is worse. But the entrepreneur who can't exit may still have a chance to fix the issues that led to the failed sale. He can potentially come back into the market and successfully sell or transfer the business.

But those who have already sold their businesses have little recourse except to nurse their wounds and in entre-preneurial speak "get some life scar tissue."

I've put these shockers into six categories. Here they are:

Purchase Price Adjusments

Working Capital Adjustments

Earn-Out Fizzle

Legal Exposure

Financial Exposure

I Got Screwed!

They Want My Savings!

Net Proceeds Gotcha

Tax Surprises

What the Heck?!

Post-Exit Shockers

No One Told Me!

Seller's Remorse

Loss of Identity

Family Conflicts

Headaches

I HATE This!

Payment Defaults

Excluded Obligations

Liquidity

Employment

No Compete

No Control

Post-Exit Shocker #1.
The "I Got Screwed!" Shocker

Ready for another dose of cold, hard truth? Here it comes.

No matter what purchase price you agree to, you probably won't get it in full.

That's because of a little something called ...

Purchase Price Adjustments

Here's how they work.

Imagine that you have a contract for the sale of your house. The buyers, after doing their inspection, come back and want reductions in selling price because they found all kinds of things wrong with the house. Maybe there are signs of water in the basement. Or maybe the furnace looks to be on its last legs.

In business, it works almost the same way except generally much worse.

Purchase price adjustments can be of all types. Some surface after the letter of intent has been signed and many after the closing has already happened.

Here are a few:

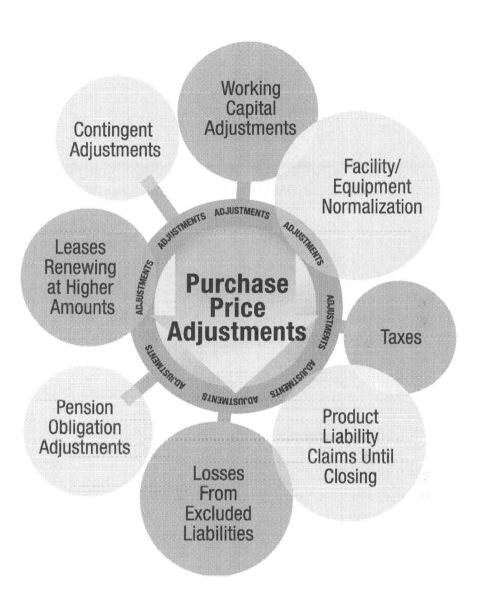

Working Capital Adjustments

When you need cash, you look at your business bank accounts, your receivables, your inventory levels and your lines of credit. That is, if you're like most entrepreneurs I know.

So let's say your normal receivables are $5,000,000 and your inventory is $1,000,000. That's $6,000,000, right?

Now, if your company has a few million or more in revenue, you are likely in for the surprise of your life. You find out that you must leave your receivables and inventory behind when you sell. The only saving grace is that you get to leave behind payables as well.

Even though middle-market companies are generally bought and sold on a cash-free, debt-free basis, the sale price includes working capital. Talk about a reality check!

And that's the kind of check you'll never be able to cash. Especially if you aren't optimizing working capital and the buyer plays games.

Working capital adjustments include:

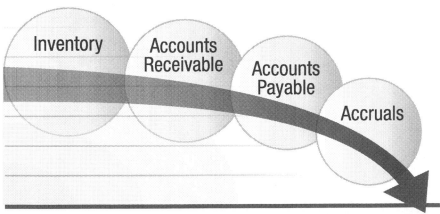

Working Capital Adjustments

Earn-Out Fizzle

I really think that the earn-out was invented by finance wizards as a clever way to get the entrepreneur to find some justification to accept the buyer's paltry valuation.

Here's what I mean.

You think your company is worth $10,000,000. The buyer thinks it is worth $5,000,000. He proposes an earn-out to bridge the valuation gap between you and the buyer.

The earn-out is based on future payments contingent on the performance of the business and is calculated using an agreed upon formula.

The problem is that many earn-outs don't materialize. In some cases, the entrepreneur was unrealistic on valuation in the first place. In other cases, the entrepreneur is naïve and simply gets taken for a ride.

Earn-outs do not materialize for all kinds of reasons. Among them …

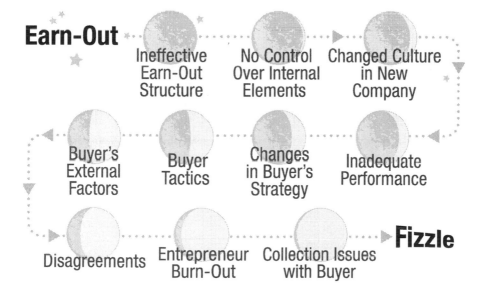

Earn-Out

Ineffective Earn-Out Structure

No Control Over Internal Elements

Changed Culture in New Company

Buyer's External Factors

Buyer Tactics

Changes in Buyer's Strategy

Inadequate Performance

Disagreements

Entrepreneur Burn-Out

Collection Issues with Buyer

Fizzle

Post-Exit Shocker #2.
The "They Want My Savings!" Shocker

Care for another cold, hard truth?

The whole process of selling a business is unfair and geared to protect the buyer. And not the entrepreneur.

Case in point. A couple of things called …

Legal and Financial Exposures

When most entrepreneurs sell their business, the last thing they think of is legal liability. Most would ask, "Legal liability for what?"

Well, there are all kinds of legal liabilities that can come back and haunt you long after you have closed and collected the proceeds of the sale.

And if you have misrepresented or not disclosed a material fact, this can create potential claims against the sale amount. You could even have exposure to claim amounts for way more than you sold the business for.

Buyers use all kinds of methods to lower their risk and put the entrepreneur on the hook. Here are some of them:

Representations & Warranties

Clawbacks

Sandbagging Claims

Set-Off Rights

Cross Default Provisions

Joint & Several Liability

Holdbacks/Escrow

Security Interests

Deferred Payments

Contingent Payments

Dispute Resolution

Litigation

**Legal & Financial
Exposures**

Post-Exit Shocker #3.
The "No One Told Me!" Shocker

Most entrepreneurs think like this:

I'll sell my company for ten million dollars. After paying taxes and debt, my take home will be seven million dollars.

Which sets them up for the dreaded …

Net Proceeds Gotcha

Net proceeds is the amount of money you will take home after paying all the taxes, debts and obligations.

The problem is that the entrepreneur's calculation of net proceeds can be very different than the real number. Most tend to oversimplify and net proceeds is anything but simple.

What makes matters worse is that most entrepreneurs have not clearly aligned their retirement cash needs with a realistic business valuation. For most entrepreneurs, their business constitutes the bulk of their net worth and that can have a huge impact on future plans. Plans for a comfortable retirement, for instance.

Here are a few of the things that can adversely affect the net proceeds calculation:

Post-Exit Shocker #4.
The "I HATE This!" Shocker

Employment and Loss of Control

One day you're the big Kahuna in your company. The next day you're an employee alongside your previous employees. Loss of control can be very devastating emotionally for the entrepreneur. Often he or she has given little thought to it and is not ready for the consequences.

Let's face it. We entrepreneurs generally are unemployable. So it's not surprising that we can't wait to leave once we've sold the company. We hate working for a larger bureaucratic organization – such as the organization that has bought our business.

Bottom line is that we don't stick around once we've sold – even if that was part of the deal. Or we have difficulties satisfying our post-closing obligations. Naturally, this costs us a lot of money.

So, why are we in a such rush to leave?

Difficulty Adjusting to Being an Employee

Personality Traits that Make Us Unemployable

Change of Company's Name

Belief Company is Headed in Wrong Direction

Employee Terminations/ Re-Shuffling

I HATE This!

Change in Company's Culture/Core Values

Elimination of Products We Created

Mishandling Long-Term Customers/ Suppliers

Post-Exit Shocker #5.
The Payment Defaults Headache

In many cases, the buyer wants the entrepreneur to provide some seller financing. But what the entrepreneur doesn't realize is that this puts him or her in a subordinated position to third-party lenders involved in financing the transaction.

That sounds like financial doubletalk. But what it means is if the company runs into trouble, the entrepreneur's security can become worthless.

Even when the entrepreneur is in a first lien position, what he doesn't realize is that he'll have to go through an extensive foreclosure process to get his business back. And in many states, sellers who have provided financing have limited recourse against the borrower if they are not paid in entirety. Besides, business assets that were pledged as security may have lost value.

Entrepreneurs have significant post-sale financial risk and it's something not to be taken lightly. Here are some:

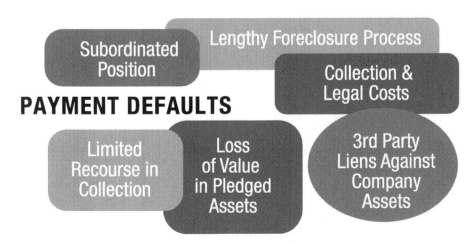

Subordinated Position

Lengthy Foreclosure Process

Collection & Legal Costs

PAYMENT DEFAULTS

Limited Recourse in Collection

Loss of Value in Pledged Assets

3rd Party Liens Against Company Assets

The Lack of Liquidity Surprise

Many of us entrepreneurs do a lousy job of managing our own finances.

We don't align them. So we can have large shortfalls when we retire because of higher than anticipated expenses, deferred payments and loss of those little owner perks we've gotten used to. This can create a severe liquidity crunch for us. Due to …

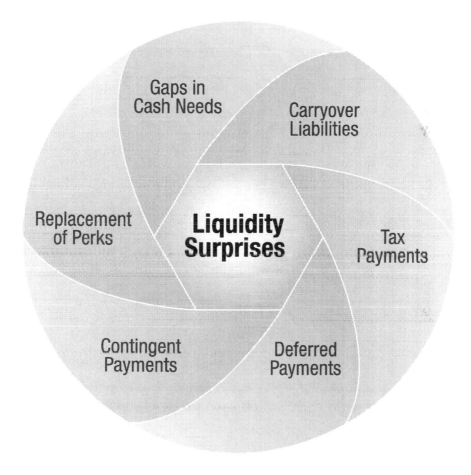

On the other hand, we might a receive sizeable chunk of cash when we sell. Most of us aren't prepared for that responsibility and we do stupid things with the money. One hears riches to rags stories all the time. Don't add yours to them.

Some of the reasons why this happens:

Post-Exit Shocker #6.
The Seller's Remorse Shocker

Most entrepreneurs simply aren't prepared emotionally for a business exit. The business has been our life for so long that we have trouble putting it behind us when we sell. This can be extremely hard for the action-oriented entrepreneur at any age and especially for the older guys and gals.

The result is often seller's remorse. As in "Why the heck did I do that?"

There are all kinds of reasons for this shocker:

A Huge
"I've Sold My Business.
What Next?"
Vacuum

Loss of
Identity

Loss of
Fulfillment

Lack
of Mental
Preparedness

Loss of
Business
Relationships:

With Suppliers

With Customers

With Colleagues

With Employees

The "Family Issues" Issue

One of the main reasons for seller remorse is that the entrepreneur is now at home full time. The spouse may not be ready for that.

The result? A new source of stress.

Other family issues arise simply because the business just sold was the family business. The spouse may be resentful because not all the children were treated equally. There also could be stress between the children who are now or previously employed by the business.

But as they say on TV, wait there's more ... more reasons family issues can contribute to seller's remorse. Such as:

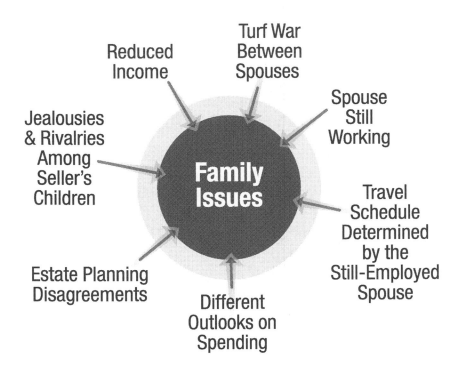

Punch me in the nose?

Well, I couldn't really blame you for wanting to do that. I've said some pretty tough things about entrepreneurs and their approach to business. You may feel that I've done everything but soap your windows and hang toilet paper on your trees. You might even believe that I've got something against entrepreneurs – even though I keep telling you that, deep down, I'm one myself.

Well, of course, I'm all for entrepreneurs. Without us, there wouldn't be a computer on your desk or in your lap … a phone in your pocket … or a car in your driveway. Neither would there be radio, TV, light bulbs, cameras or just about any of the things that make life better. All those things were invented by and made possible by … wait for it … entrepreneurs.

So please don't get the idea that you've got to give up the qualities that make you an entrepreneur … your willingness to take risks … your spirit of independence … your commitment to hard work … and all the rest.

What I'm trying to do is to show you the qualities you need to add in order to get your business ready to sell for top dollar and how to add them.

That's what the next part of the book is all about. I'm going to show you how to defuse that damned Exit Bomb.

You won't need a blast suit. But you might want to skip that cup of coffee.

Defusing a bomb requires a steady hand.

Before We Go Any Further

Wondering how you'd do if you had to exit your company right away? Find out with a complimentary Exit Bomb Readiness Score™ at www.ExitBomb.Org/Score.

Just answer a few questions online and we'll share a report to help you gauge your own readiness for exit.

Part II.
Defusing the Exit Bomb

Chapter 7.
Cash is the Problem

Even though I'd been one for most of my life, I decided that a good start to writing this book would be to look up the meaning of the word "entrepreneur."

It comes from a French word. I'd already guessed that much. The word is *"entreprendre"* which means, "to undertake."

I checked out the Oxford Dictionary and found it defined as "A person who organizes and operates a business or businesses, taking on greater than normal financial risks in order to do so."

Between these two definitions, I had a revelation.

Pretty much since the first entrepreneur, many of us who followed were doomed to enslaving ourselves to our businesses while taking on greater than normal risks without any regard to the investment return.

No wonder we have such a hard time selling our businesses for what they're worth!

That's the disconnect between the entrepreneur and the buyer; the reason we either can't sell our businesses or sell them for chicken feed.

Most buyers are investors and focused on value. They will spend money and effort with the expectation of achieving a profit while minimizing all kinds of risks.

We entrepreneurs, on the other hand, are idea people — focused on bringing an idea to market. We will spend money and effort to turn that idea into a business that supports our lifestyle and financial objectives. All with little to no regard for any kind of risk.

This is a major disconnect between the buyer and the entrepreneur, and it has a clear source.

Most entrepreneurs are focused on cash generation.

NOT value creation.

Buyers, on the other hand, are focused on value creation. Cash generation is simply a pre-requisite. Table stakes, in other words.

The fault doesn't necessarily lay with us entrepreneurs. The chips are stacked against us from the beginning.

When we start, the rules are simple. Get off your butt. Go get it done. Don't take no for an answer. There's always a way. Do what needs to be done.

In the process of building our businesses, we make tremendous sacrifices. We borrow money, pay exorbitantly high interest rates, forego vacations, deplete savings and deal with tremendous amounts of stress and crap. And, in many cases, we don't do this alone. Our significant others and children are along for the ride.

From day one, we are worried about cash flow. That is the lifeline. Right?

We are always chasing cash for all kinds of business needs: Payroll, inventory, working capital, capital expenditures, paying down lines of credit and taxes. And don't forget the iPad for the kiddo, braces for the other kiddo and the new sofa that will get bought whether you like it or not.

In other words, for the entrepreneur:

CASH = SURVIVAL

We are hard-wired to generate cash. This is our biggest strength and the biggest weakness.

We do this cash generation in a mental cocoon with little to no regard to creating sustainable value in our companies. In other words: A business that can thrive without us.

If we get the business to operate independently of ourselves we can get a handsome reward, and if it can't, we pay the price. By that, I mean we can't sell or we sell our life's work for a big discount while holding our noses.

When it comes to exits, our weakness does not stop at our focus on cash generation alone.

As I discussed in Detonator #1 (Entrepreneur Factors), most of us have personality traits, qualities and strengths that one must have to be a successful entrepreneur. These work against the entrepreneur in an exit.

The buyer's perspective of what creates value is very different from ours. We manage our companies to maximize cash flow and generally not to mitigate risk. The buyer focuses not just on cash flow but also on the potential return on investment.

So, what needs to change?

Well, let's start from the top down.

Let's change our MINDSET.

Chapter 8.

Evolving the Entrepreneur Mindset

To evolve our mindset into one that will actually help us exit successfully, we must deal with the identity issue.

By that I mean that, for most of us, the business becomes our identity. It is difficult for us to separate ourselves from our business.

How tied is your identity to your business?

Many entrepreneurs call their business their "baby." What about yours?

That may be all well and good but if you're trying to sell your business, it's a problem.

It starts in the beginning, when the business needs the entrepreneur to be involved in everything. Pretty soon, the business becomes the entrepreneur and vice versa.

As the business grows and employees are added, the entrepreneur still doesn't give up the tactical role. Rather than employees executing the entrepreneur's vision, the business still revolves around the entrepreneur's tactical involvement.

This is a key mindset issue and, in my humble opinion, one

of the key reasons why so many entrepreneurs cannot sell or maximize the exit value of their companies. We create a situation where:

Our businesses can't exist without us.

Having dealt with all kinds of buyers, there's one thing I can tell you: They don't like to buy businesses that can't operate without the owners. Either they will walk away or they will want a significant discount or really favorable terms to get the deal done.

I ask you:

Would you rather be in control or rich?

So, how do you fix that? How do you change your mindset?

To start:

Remember that your business is an asset.
It isn't your identity.

It is simply something you created. It is an asset that can be bought and sold. The faster you get into an asset-oriented mindset, the easier your life will be on many levels.

1. You will be more objective about your business as a business and its viability and sustainability.

2. You will be more objective about its value as an asset.

When I'm working with companies to substantially enhance their value, I often have the entrepreneur do a visualization exercise, because this picture really says it all.

Entrepreneur

Switch Places

Business

My point is that we make our business the "mothership" and ourselves the little "fighter craft."

It isn't surprising. We are used to be being subservient to our businesses. Our lives revolve around them.

Well, become the mothership. Make the business one of the smaller crafts. If one blows up or is sold, it does not impact the mothership, which can still continue.

Switch places, evolve your mindset and you will see all kinds of dividends. You might even be happier.

Remember, it's OK to love your business. Just don't live your business.

By the way, this change in mindset will allow you to start doing what needs to be done to start enhancing your business asset so it can be sold one day for maximum value.

Otherwise, the mothership could become your death star.

Value and Risk

Exit Bomb. Why Most Entrepreneurs Can't Sell, Don't Sell or Sell Their Company For Peanuts.

Chapter 9.

Understanding What Creates Value in a Company

Clients always ask me, "Gower, what do you think my company is worth?" and I always smile and say the same thing: "What exit channel do you want to choose?" I normally get a blank stare, as in "What do you mean?"

I mean just that. Every exit channel – whether you want to sell internally to employees or transfer ownership to your family members or sell externally to third parties – has its own specific valuation, tax implications and channel specific liabilities and exposures.

This diagram shows how different exit channels use different valuation methods and, as a result, can have a wide range of company valuations for the very same company.

Exit Channel	Valuation Method	Valuation
Internal Buy/Sell	Asset Value	$4.2MM
Management Buy-Out	Investment Value	$7.9MM
Employee Stock Ownership Plan	Fair Market Value	$10.8MM
Recapitalization	Financial Market Value	$13.8MM
Competitive/Private Auction	Synergized Market Value	$18.1MM
IPO	Public Market Value	Unknown

As entrepreneurs, we tend to split our organizations into functional areas. An example of this would be sales, marketing, finance, employees etc.

But when it comes to maximizing exit value, we need to think in terms of "multiple transfers of value" to achieve maximum sale price.

I have laid these "transfers of value" out in five categories and call them the "5 Transfers to Maximize Valuation." In most cases, some or all of these have to come together for you to get the maximum value for your company.

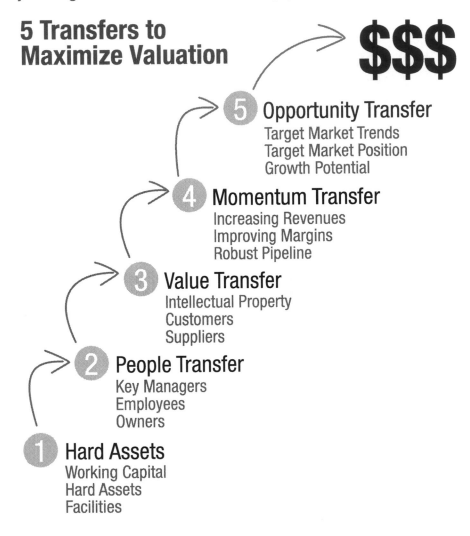

5 Transfers to Maximize Valuation

$$$

⑤ Opportunity Transfer
Target Market Trends
Target Market Position
Growth Potential

④ Momentum Transfer
Increasing Revenues
Improving Margins
Robust Pipeline

③ Value Transfer
Intellectual Property
Customers
Suppliers

② People Transfer
Key Managers
Employees
Owners

① Hard Assets
Working Capital
Hard Assets
Facilities

If I ask you what creates value in a company, you'd probably say increasing revenues, increasing cash and increasing profits.

I agree with you. These create tremendous value. From the buyer's perspective, however, they are prerequisites to the game, and that isn't all the buyer will look at.

If you have a company that has ten million dollars in revenue and has amazing gross margins and great cash flow but the revenue relies too heavily on one customer who could have a heart attack tomorrow, that is not necessarily the buyer's idea of value.

As I said earlier, the entrepreneur is hard-wired to generate cash. Everything revolves around exactly that. There is little to no regard for any other value driver. And that's a mistake.

The diagram shows some variables beyond revenue and profits that can increase or decrease the value of a company.

Market Position	Diversity: Customers, Suppliers & Products	Financial Transparency
Competitive Advantage		Growth Opportunities
	Management Depth & Breadth	Well Maintained Facilities & Equipment
Barriers to Entry	Business Model	
Useful Life of Patents	Intellectual Property	Strength of Sales Force

We entrepreneurs want the highest premium for our businesses when we sell but we don't understand that, from the buyer's perspective, paying a premium for a company generally involves a balance between risk reduction, growth potential and financing leverage.

Here are some examples of what increases value even more:

What Increases Value Even Higher?

Reduction of Risk	+	Growth Potential	+	Financing Leverage
Transaction Terms		Synergies		Low CAPEX
Financial Transparency		Target Market Growth		Cost of Capital
Recurring Revenue		Market Position		Stable Cash Flows
Customer Diversity		Momentum		
Contracts with Key Players		Realistic Growth Plan		

The selling multiple can go up if the buyer can reduce his risk in all kinds of ways.

The buyer can accomplish this by shifting risk to the seller using transaction terms and conditions.

Or by buying a company with stable cash flows, customer diversity and a realistic growth plan.

Or by using financing leverage on a company with an asset and working capital-light business.

Remember, the buyer brings the multiple, and the multiple

depends very much on cost of capital as well as synergies and/or undervalued or disruptive intellectual property.

Another point of confusion is the difference between value and price. Value is calculated. It is calculated using future earning potential and reduction of risk.

Price is negotiated. Price will increase or decrease based on transaction structure, shifting of risk between buyer and seller, the motivation of the buyer, the buyer cost of capital and other factors.

Value vs. Price

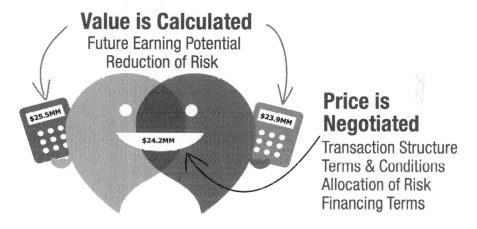

Value is Calculated
Future Earning Potential
Reduction of Risk

$25.5MM

$24.2MM

$23.9MM

Price is Negotiated
Transaction Structure
Terms & Conditions
Allocation of Risk
Financing Terms

Maximizing your selling price will depend on you knowing what the buyer wants.

Have another look at the "5 Transfers to Maximize Valuation" graphic in this chapter.

Maximum Sale Price = Optimal (Assets + People + Value + Momentum + Opportunity)

Unless you are lucky and have something that a buyer must have regardless of your company state of affairs, you will need to optimize these five transfers to get a premium for your life's hard work.

Chapter 10.

Valuation: Entrepreneur vs. Buyer

Stop me if you've heard this before … we entrepreneurs have a major value disconnect with market reality. We are heavily influenced by the high dollar exit stories we hear on the news all the time. Of course, it's our nature to think the impossible and be super-optimistic but, at the same time, we need to understand the perils of over-optimism.

Entrepreneurs are big picture, big idea people. We hatch an idea. We bring it to market. We go get results. We generate cash flow. Years go by and we want to sell.

Then comes the big question: *"What is my business worth?"*

And in comes the barrage of ways to value a business. The academics have done a good job with highly technical, all-encompassing books on valuations but there is a serious lack of simple and easy to understand material for the entrepreneur.

The following is my humble effort to help you understand the valuation landscape and why the valuation gap between the buyer and seller happens. Considering this is one of the biggest reasons that exits fail, I hope you will give this perspective plenty of attention.

No one has the magic formula on valuation. If you get yourself a valuation, take it with a grain of salt. There is a huge difference between traditional valuations done for compliance purposes (like estate planning or getting a loan) and a valuation for selling your business.

In the mergers and acquisitions world, formal valuations have limited applicability. The M&A valuation will be based on multiple factors like comparable transactions in the marketplace, cost of capital, financial engineering by the buyer, cost or revenue synergies being realized by the buyer etc.

If the buyer is using financial arbitrage or valuation multiple arbitrage, his purchase price may be entirely different than somebody who is not relying on that strategy.

A public company that trades at a P/E of 22 can, in many cases, afford to pay more than market value of a private company because in the next quarter when they report earnings, most of the acquired cash stream will trade at the public company multiple.

Another example of arbitrage is when a private equity firm buys a company using a consolidation strategy, in the hope that the size results in a larger multiple.

My point is that valuations often exist in a cocoon — especially in the absence of a buyer. Once the buyer has been identified, it is imperative to understand the buyer's buying motivation and potential of realized synergies in order to negotiate a higher purchase price.

I will tell you one truth that holds true for an overwhelming majority of entrepreneurs.

The entrepreneur's view of his or her company's value is VERY different from the buyer's view of value.

In fact, an overwhelming majority of merger and

acquisition advisors think that their clients have unrealistic expectations of their company's value.

So why are so many of us completely out of touch with market reality which, in turn, gives us unnecessary surprises?

Why is it that we, as entrepreneurs, can't seem to be objective about the exit multiple?

Well, part of this is that we are opportunistic optimists and we try to maximize any situation we are put into.

It also has to do with multiple factors that have nothing to do with the actual market value of the business.

In my research and experience, the entrepreneur's unrealistic selling price expectations can be lumped into three mindsets about value.

1. Sacrifice Value: Entrepreneurs often borrow on credit cards, sign personal guarantees, take on tremendous amounts of debt, work long hours, and make incredible sacrifices to launch and grow their businesses. The sacrifices don't stop with them. Often their families, parents, spouses, children, friends and others sacrifice along with the entrepreneur. And are, in many cases, equally invested in the turmoil and turbulence that results from entrepreneurship.

Because of the sacrifices we make, we're often unrealistic on the price of the business. We equate "sweat equity" with the value of the business, making it, in our mind, more valuable than the market reality. This creates a tremendous amount of pain when we discover that the business value is much lower than what we had imagined.

Worse, most entrepreneurs have more than 80% of their net worth invested in their companies. This creates an expectation gap and makes the entrepreneur unrealistic about price. Often the business has been given priority in the hope of an eventual sale and cash out in an "umbrella exit" scenario. (By "umbrella exit," I mean relaxing on a beach with a drink with an umbrella in it.)

2. The E-Math Value: This is where the entrepreneur takes the potential sale proceeds, adjusts for taxes and debts and then puts it in a bank account yielding some nominal interest rate to see if they can replace his or her lifestyle on that income.

Annual Income Before Sale:	**$1,000,000**
Multiple:	5X
Purchase Price:	$5,000,000
Taxes & Debt:	$2,000,000
Net Take Home Investable Cash:	$3,000,000
Entrepreneur's Investment Income After Sale @ 4% Interest:	**$120,000**

vs.

In the example, if you are the entrepreneur and see you'll have to adjust from making a million dollars a year to trying to live on $120,000 annually, everything just stops there. This is what happens when we look at lifestyle and income as the deciding factors regardless of what's happening in the market.

In many cases, this mindset keeps the entrepreneur holding on until it is way too late to sell.

In other cases, entrepreneurs take the financial number they think they'll need for retirement and make that their business value. For example, "If I need $5 million for retirement, then my expectation of value of my business is $5 million regardless of market reality."

3. Opportunity Value: This is a classic case of drinking too much of our own Kool-Aid. We entrepreneurs are generally very optimistic and passionate about our companies and our products. Entrepreneurs love to talk in terms of percentages. You may hear something like:

"We only need to get 3% of the market and this will be a billion dollar company."

Unfortunately, the entrepreneur's optimism is often not matched with reality. Being bullish on his company's growth prospects is one thing, but often their passion for the market opportunity is not in sync with the internal capabilities of their organization. It is almost certainly not in touch with the working capital needs and capital expenditures required to realize highly optimistic growth goals.

When the entrepreneur sits across from the buyer and shares this massive opportunity, he or she is really focused on one side of the picture – which is the opportunity itself.

However, the buyer has a more objective lens and is not just looking at the market opportunity but also the company's actual capacity to harvest the opportunity. The buyer wants to make sure that the growth opportunity is realistic and takes into account the need for increases in working capital and capital expenditures, etc. This creates a big disconnect between the buyer and the seller.

What entrepreneurs often forget is that buyers are investors. They are essentially buying the entrepreneur's company as an investment. They have an asset-oriented mindset. Their goal may be to acquire your company to realize synergies and/or to increase its value and sell it a few years later for a fat profit.

Twenty years ago I went to a venture capital conference.

I needed to raise money for my own business and I remember a venture capitalist on a panel said this:

> *"When it comes to entrepreneurs, we know your financials are bullshit; we just want to know the magnitude of your bullshit."*

That line has stayed with me and I use it often. The point I'm trying to make is that your buyers are investors and they will peel away the bullshit factor from the opportunity, and they will bring it down to the reality of your growth plan and capabilities of your organization.

They will also vet it against their own business mandates and capabilities. And by the time they apply their process, there will likely be a big valuation gap between entrepreneur and the buyer.

Valuation vs. Real Worth

The problem is that most entrepreneurs don't understand the difference between valuation and real worth. What entrepreneurs almost never seem to realize is that their initial valuation is almost always preliminary. When the buyer starts looking under the hood in the business, that valuation gets adjusted for inefficiencies, deficiencies, errors, obligations, liabilities and risks.

These adjustments will translate into "real worth." That is, what your company is actually worth to the buyer after he adjusts for all kinds of things. This actual worth is what the entrepreneur must accept or walk away from the transaction.

It's no different than buying a house. Let's say that you offer $900,000 for a house. The inspection comes back with a laundry list of items that need to be fixed. You demand that the seller take $75,000 off the purchase price to fix all the problems. The $900,000 was a preliminary valuation and $825,000 ($900,000 less $75,000) is the actual price you're willing to pay for the home. That's the difference between valuation and real worth.

The other problem is that the entrepreneur, in many cases, has limited visibility into what the true inefficiencies, deficiencies, errors, obligations, liabilities and risks are within his business. These can range from revenue recognition issues and over-reliance on the entrepreneur to customer concentrations and non-operating liabilities.

On the other hand, the buyer's view of value is very simple. He will leverage negatives to drive down the purchase price. When this happens, the entrepreneur can get quite emotional and can be in a state of denial. Often this is a huge reason the exit transaction doesn't get done.

OK, now I'm going to take a crack at translating all the academic stuff on the subject into the three most common ways to value a business.

1. Market Approach: This looks at comparable transactions in the marketplace and tries to determine a value based on what's happening within the market.

2. Income Approach: This takes into account the income of your assets/business. In doing so it will look at both the expense side as well as the revenue generated. The income stream is then discounted to come to a present-day value.

3. Cost Approach: This is very focused on the expense for replacing or reproducing the company's assets and their underlying depreciation.

At the end of the day, the valuation will be determined with buyer and seller negotiations. M&A advisors and valuation experts will validate price by looking at the market as well as comparable transactions (also known as comps).

It takes optimism to be an entrepreneur; it takes realism to sell a business. Determining the value of your company will be less about textbook formulas and more about what you can convince a buyer to pay for it.

Whether you are ready to sell now or have a long-term horizon, it's best to take a hard look at your business – the same sort of hard look your potential buyers will be taking.

It is highly advisable that you work with a competent advisor to determine a realistic valuation range for your business before even contemplating the sale process. This will greatly minimize surprises and improve the outcome. It will be worth every penny.

Chapter 11.

How Growth Can Hurt Sale Valuation

Growth ... for lack of a better word ... is "good." Right?

Well, not so fast there.

Most of us assume that a high-growth company is a high-value company. While that may generally be the case, I am here to tell you that growth can hurt exit value as well.

Your selling price will likely be a multiple of your EBITDA (earnings before interest, taxes, depreciation and amortization). Except, there's one huge problem with EBITDA.

EBITDA ignores working capital and capital expenditures. Case in point: You can be a very profitable company and have no cash. It is likely that your cash is sitting in accounts receivable, inventory, work in process etc. It is quite common for me to run across businesses with substantial revenues as well as substantial profits but absolutely no cash.

For many companies, depending on your cash conversion cycle, the faster you grow, the higher your working capital and capital expenditure (CAPEX) needs. (Capital expenditures are the monies you spend to purchase or upgrade fixed assets.) It is entirely possible that if you aren't paying careful attention to your cash deficit and don't have adequate financing, you could go out of business.

This is where cash becomes a problem at selling time.

Even though your valuation would likely be a multiple of your EBITDA, the reality is that the buyer is most likely looking at your free cash flow (FCF). The reason is that FCF generally takes into account the increases in working capital to finance your growth.

This is a key number for the buyer. If you've got a business that requires a lot of annual recurring capital expenditure to grow and/or has a long cash conversion cycle requiring substantial working capital, there's a decent likelihood that the buyer could want a significant discount or will walk away.

Why?

Simply put: A typical buyer doesn't want to buy a business that requires heavy annual capital expenditure investment or substantial additional working capital. The buyer is likely already borrowing heavily to pay the purchase price.

If the buyer has to come up with millions of dollars in addition for capital expenditures annually as well as provide liquidity to fund significant working capital shortfalls, that requires him to borrow additional money. Unless you've got something that they really, really need, most buyers tend to not look at this favorably. Or, if they do buy, they will significantly reduce the valuation multiple.

I get inquiries all the time from various professional investors looking for the right type of "asset-light and/or working capital-light or innovation-light" business.

Translation: The buyer doesn't want to have to make substantial additional investments in the business because, if they do, they have to borrow more and this lowers their rate of return.

If your company is one where there is a long cash conversion cycle requiring significant increases in working capital or heavy annual capital expenditures, your best bet would be to sell to a strategic acquirer with deep pockets who is more focused on the opportunity than the immediate financial economies. (The cash conversion cycle, or CCC, is a cash flow calculation that measures the time a business takes to convert its investment in inventory and other resources into cash. In simple words, it is a measure of how long your cash is tied up in the business before something can be sold and cash collected from the customer.)

In selling, high-growth companies need to make sure they line up cash to survive the "sell the business" cycle. A classic horror story is when the company is in high-growth mode and bleeding cash. The company has a few months of operating capital left before it needs to raise more cash. In comes a buyer with a decent offer to buy. The seller knows he will need cash in a few months but doesn't want to start the capital acquisition process with third parties when there is a buyer interested.

Negotiations start, due diligence begins. The seller is in a rush; the buyer is not. The seller is running out of cash and the buyer senses this and renegotiates price downward during due diligence. The poor seller is in a hostage situation. If he doesn't accept, his company could go bankrupt.

Other problems could surface for growth companies.

Buyers carefully look at maintenance capital expenditures vs. growth capital expenditures. Very simply, maintenance CAPEX is a cost. Growth CAPEX is an investment.

Often the entrepreneur has a tax reduction mindset and will try to deduct capital expenses by marking them as operating expenses. All is well until it comes time to sell and the financials are recast. This is where the entrepreneur and buyer dance will begin.

The entrepreneur and his advisors will claim that many of these expenses were actually growth-related capital expenditures (growth CAPEX) and not maintenance expenses (maintenance CAPEX). The buyer will generally fight tooth and nail, claiming otherwise. He doesn't want to be shortchanged and left saddled with unknown recurring expenditures.

Let's say you were incurring $300,000 annually in growth CAPEX but you are marking $100,000 as maintenance-related expenses to get your taxes down. You are essentially setting a precedent that you need $100,000 a year to maintain your facilities and equipment.

This becomes a sticky point with the buyer if you try to claim that this was really not the case because many of these items were, in fact, growth CAPEX. Also, keep in mind that by deducting many of the growth CAPEX-related items you have likely depressed your earnings. The problem becomes magnified when there is a multiplier effect.

$100,000 X 6= $600,000.

Assuming the buyer's valuation multiple is six times your EBITDA, you can end up giving a nice $600,000 purchase price subsidy to the buyer or you can walk away. Either way, it won't make for a fun day.

In many cases, the entrepreneur has little to no visibility into this issue because of the sheer size of the transactions going through the company. If the entrepreneur has inflated his maintenance CAPEX to get taxes down, it benefits the buyer and the buyer is not likely to tip his hand.

There are other ways CAPEX impacts your valuation. Growth companies are almost always hemorrhaging cash and in some cases don't have the capital to properly maintain assets. They can have a significant amount of deferred maintenance on equipment and facilities.

It's very likely the buyer will normalize these capital expenditures and this will end up reducing the purchase price.

I usually suggest to clients that they track capital expenditures diligently and create different accounts: one for maintenance CAPEX and another for growth CAPEX. That will provide a real look into what the actual profitability of the company actually is.

Remember, maintenance CAPEX is an expense and that's your problem. Growth CAPEX is an investment and it's the buyer's problem. The logic behind this is that if the company decides to stop investing in growth, the growth CAPEX would be substantially reduced, resulting in more cash that would be available for other uses.

That said; smart buyers are constantly trying to put growth CAPEX into the maintenance CAPEX bucket. Being prepared in advance and having visibility into your CAPEX will save you a nosebleed.

Another area that comes into play is the product mix impact on value. Many entrepreneurs invest blindly in growth. In some cases, cash streams from different revenue segments may get valued differently.

Let's say you are a manufacturer looking to grow. Using an adjacency strategy, you decide to get into a complimentary product or service line. At exit time, you may find that the value of your core product business is very different than your extension product business. This can help or hurt your valuation depending on your situation.

For example, a commercial cleaning business that decides to start selling supplies to customers may increase its value. While a glass manufacturer that makes glass for cellular phones but diversifies revenues by manufacturing glass for windowpanes may negatively impact its value.

Is growth good? It all depends.

Growth is a two-edged sword. While growth is mission critical, your company's growth alone will likely not secure a high valuation. Strong growth is often accompanied by various elements that can increase the long-term risk of failure. There are hidden costs and risks in growth that the entrepreneur might ignore and a potential buyer will focus on.

Having a $30,000,000 revenue company with infrastructure and systems suitable for a $3,000,000 company may require substantial additional reinvestment dollars, as well an extended time frame, before it can grow further. This will most likely reduce exit value.

Besides, smart buyers will ignore simple measures of revenue and earnings growth, and focus instead on your company's free cash flow and future CAPEX needs to determine a realistic valuation multiple.

Chapter 12.

How Synergies Affect Valuation

The entrepreneur decides one day to sell his business. He figures he'll find a broker and then list the business for sale. Simple, right?

Well, that's one way to do it. If the entrepreneur has a decent business there is a reasonable chance it will sell. However, our entrepreneur will also be leaving a lot of money on the table.

The reason our entrepreneur won't be able to maximize exit value is that the word "synergy" is off his or her radar. Most entrepreneurs don't understand the concept and certainly are not leveraging the true advantage of a synergistic sale.

It's quite common for entrepreneurs to sell to the first buyer who approaches them. The buyer comes in, starts talking to the entrepreneur and, if there's good rapport between the buyer and the entrepreneur, it seems natural to extend that conversation with a letter of intent. Pretty soon the entrepreneur is knee deep in due diligence and negotiating a purchase and sale agreement.

It's kind of like dating and asking the first person you go out with to marry you.

Most entrepreneurs don't have the inclination to go out and search for synergistic buyers who would pay a pretty penny for the entrepreneur's company. I don't know if this is because the entrepreneur is just being lazy, unwilling to do the heavy lifting of finding multiple buyers interested in the company or due to lack of knowledge.

No matter what the reason, it results in a tremendous amount of the entrepreneur's wealth being lost. I always tell my clients that, in most cases, "One buyer is NO buyer."

Buyers generally buy businesses on the basis of their underlying cash flow. Therefore, it is imperative that you shift the dialogue away from the buyer paying you for a multiple of your cash flow to a multiple of the actual opportunity.

Remember, buyers are there to expand their business and to create value for their shareholders. They will pay extra if they can uncover an opportunity, which, if properly taken advantage of, could create additional shareholder value.

Why would a buyer pay 8x for a business with a market value of 5x? There has to be some justification to do that. There has to be a synergy that justifies the premium the buyer would pay above and beyond the market value.

Synergy can generate higher returns by leveraging a merged company vs. a company by itself.

Another way to look at a synergistic view is:

1 + 1 = 3

Synergies could be of various types. Generally, you will hear about cost and revenue synergies. To explain the concept better, I am splitting synergies a bit deeper.

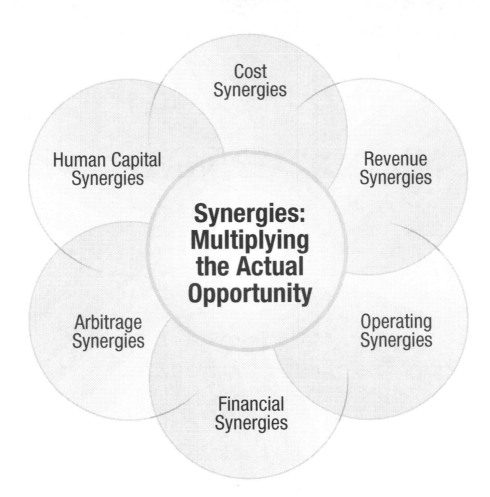

Cost Synergies: These synergies are focused on cost reduction. These could be reduced overhead in production, a reduction of head count, increased purchasing power (which drives down cost of goods sold), elimination of redundant expenses and consolidation of infrastructure.

Revenue Synergies: These synergies are focused on increasing top-line revenue by adding complimentary products and services, cross-selling of products and services, access to new markets, improved time to market by shortening the research and development cycle, and increased revenue growth by eliminating and/or reducing competition.

Operating Synergies: These generally result from increased pricing power by reducing competition and consolidating different types of functional strengths, such as combining a great product with newly acquired distribution channels.

Financial Synergies: These can result from achieving tax benefits using certain laws and consolidating operations to increase debt capacity.

Arbitrage Synergies: These may result from combining two entities to increase size because larger size generally leads to a higher multiple. Another example would be a public entity buying a private entity and absorbing the purchased company's earnings into its own and benefitting from the arbitrage. For example, buying a company for 6x while the public entity trades for 17x.

Human Capital Synergies: This is where your company gets acquired because the buyer simply wants your human capital assets, i.e. your people. This is especially prevalent in technology acquisitions.

Synergies will also depend on whether the buyer's business motive is based on a horizontal vs. a vertical acquisition strategy.

A buyer with a horizontal-integration strategy can realize significant synergies by eliminating redundant expenses and increasing revenues by absorbing a similar customer base.

A vertical-integration strategy generally involves the realization of a specific business goal. An example of this would be to strengthen the supply chain by buying up an important supplier. Many times vertical acquisition strategies are used as an indirect way to control or limit supplies in the marketplace. Typically, that's to keep these supplies out of the hands of the competition.

Synergistic buyers may be willing to pay more but they are extremely astute. They will negotiate hard. In order to get the optimum price when I am presenting a client company to buyers, I often show them three EBITDAs.

EBITDA 1: The EBITDA as it exists in the entrepreneur's company without recasting.

EBITDA 2: The recast EBITDA, which includes a host of add backs like one time and non-recurring expenses etc.

EBITDA 3: The synergized EBITDA. This EBITDA is focused on quantifying and presenting to the buyer the synergies she will realize by acquiring my client's company.

Once we start a dialogue with the buyer, we do careful analysis in order to understand the buyer's true motivation.

While we're confident that, no matter what the estimate of synergies we have calculated, there is a good chance our estimate is wrong. However, we have shifted the dialogue away from a multiple of cash flow to a multiple of the real opportunities in my client's company.

That said; buyers don't generally react well to the synergized EBITDA. They will start a barrage of reasons of why our calculations are wrong. I like to ask them what they think the correct calculation is.

If they engage in this of type conversation, I always chuckle to myself because in doing so, they are acknowledging that the purchase price would likely be based on a variation of the synergized EBITDA. Although the buyer will try to deflect, evade and change the dialogue, in many cases a compromise can be found that can drive the multiple up. In other cases, however, it is a futile exercise.

Time is a big factor in identifying, profiling and analyzing synergistic buyers. Finding one is hard but well worth the effort.

Smart entrepreneurs and their advisors must do the upfront work to understand how a potential buyer could benefit from the selling company to realize maximum value.

Instead of sending some email or flier to the buyer, a phone call that helps the buyer visualize the opportunity has always worked well for me.

A call would go something like this:

"I see that you recently acquired XYZ company. I have a client, company ABC, that can add tremendous value. Here is why ..."

The point is that the buyer may not have thought of that angle or may not be aware of the opportunity and its potential at all. It doesn't hurt to get them thinking in this direction.

Besides, in order to get top dollar, your company must represent an opportunity for the buyer to convert something they already have, be it management expertise, idle capital, industry experience or something else, into strong investment returns.

Chapter 13.

Understanding How Risk Affects Value

Ask entrepreneurs "What adds risks to a business?"

Most will answer, "Debt."

While that's true, it's just one variable. What's interesting is that entrepreneurs never look at their businesses as risky. Which explains why many entrepreneurs have difficulty answering this question. The entrepreneur is generally not wired to think in terms of risk. This is why the bulk of small businesses and many middle market companies have difficulty selling.

There are a lot of lifestyle entrepreneurs with little to no exit strategy. Their companies may generate plenty of cash but the business itself has minimal or no saleable value.

If you look up the definition of risk you will find something like, "potential of losing something of value weighed against the potential of gaining something of value."

OK, that's a somewhat bookish view of what risk is. I know that skydiving is very risky. This is why I refuse to do it. Ha!

Let me redefine risk in terms of exiting your business.

How about this?

Lowering risk gives you the ability to increase your business's value without actually increasing its revenues or profits.

That's why it's so important to focus on what risk actually is — and not just any kind of risk. Let's look at risk from the buyer's perspective.

There's usually a wide gap between how the buyer and seller view risk.

The buyer puts risk in several separate categories:

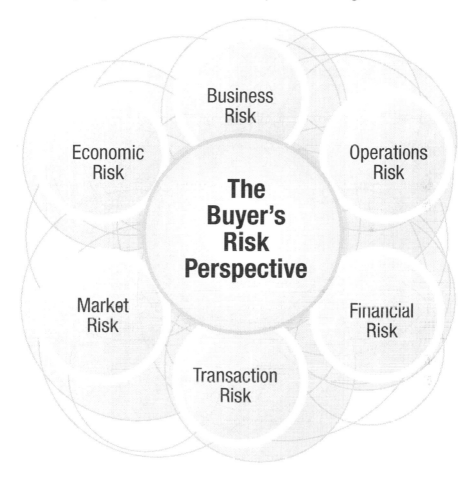

The entrepreneur on the other hand does not even think in these risk categories. Most don't think of their businesses as being risky and many can be quite oblivious to risk.

What increases risk: There are numerous elements that the buyer will view as risky. Examples of this include:

Business Risk

Non-Proprietary Products/ Technology

Commoditized Products

Low Margins/ Lower than Industry Margins

Bid Type/ Selling Opportunities

Operational Risks

Concentrations

No Barriers to Entry

Inefficiencies

Talent Gaps

Financial Risk

Inconsistent Revenues & Margins

Flat Revenue Growth

Declining Revenues & Margins

Declining Order Backlog

Transaction Risk

Deal Structure

Terms & Conditions

Non-Compete/ Non-Solicit Agreements

Payment Terms

Market Risks

Foreign Competition

Declining Valuations

Obsolescence

Changes in Legislation

Economic Risks

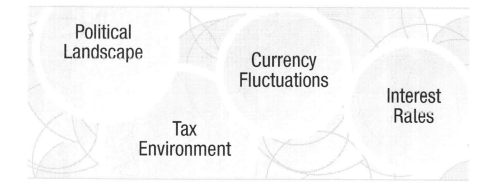

Political Landscape

Currency Fluctuations

Interest Rates

Tax Environment

What decreases risk? There are all kinds of elements that reduce risk. However, there are certain ones that buyers like to focus on. They see them as critical to decreasing risk in a business. Some examples can be seen in the following graphics:

Diversity

Financial Stability

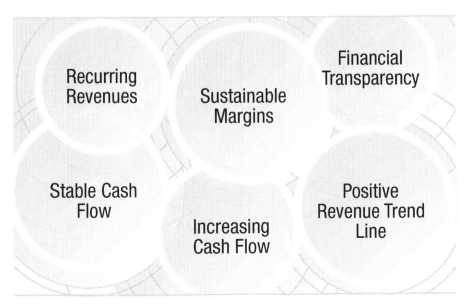

Current Position

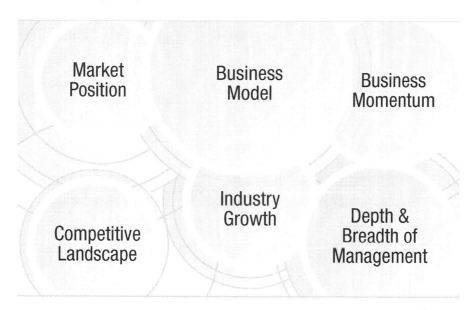

Market Position

Business Model

Business Momentum

Competitive Landscape

Industry Growth

Depth & Breadth of Management

Defensibility of Market Position

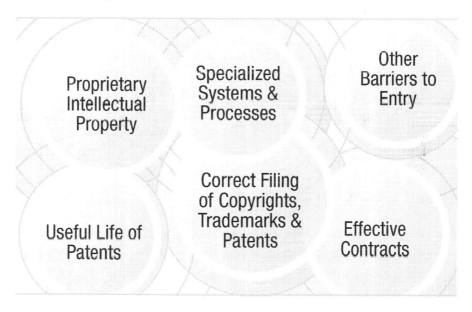

Proprietary Intellectual Property

Specialized Systems & Processes

Other Barriers to Entry

Useful Life of Patents

Correct Filing of Copyrights, Trademarks & Patents

Effective Contracts

The entrepreneur is focused on getting earnings up because he or she anticipates a multiple of earnings. While that's important, the problem is that there is no focus on risk at all. And often, this can dramatically impact exit valuation.

Let's say you're doing $10,000,000 in revenue and $2,000,000 in profits but the revenue is highly dependent on you, the entrepreneur. Then, by chance, you become incapacitated. Customers jump ship, banks pull their lines of credit, key employees leave with some big customers and your competitors pounce on the rest.

Odds are the business won't survive and if it does, its value will be severely hampered. This is a classic example of an entrepreneurial company and risk. Good revenues, great lifestyle and yet not sustainable.

Or let's take the same company – $10,000,000 in revenue and $2,000,000 in profit. You are humming along and a competitor comes up with a new technology, which delivers what you do at half the cost and with better speed.

Your business may die slowly or fast. Either way, my message is the same: Just because you have good revenues does not mean that you don't have significant risks within your company.

Risk is difficult to measure, which is why you must understand what risks potential buyers will see within your company. This will allow you to proactively prepare and rectify key concerns.

Reduction of risk is a big valuation enhancement opportunity for entrepreneurs. Those that focus on creating a balance between revenue generation and risk reduction are more likely to be handsomely rewarded by buyers.

Chapter 14.

Understanding the Buyer

The first thing you need to know is that whatever your reason for wanting to exit your business, it is almost always entirely different from the buyer's motivation to buy the business.

Regardless of each party's motivation, there's one thing that's crystal clear: The buyer is not really buying a business; they are buying a business opportunity.

The buyer will almost certainly look at your historical cash flows but what he's really buying is the promise of tomorrow. In order for this promise of tomorrow to materialize, the buyer will take a deep look into the viability, sustainability and reality of the growth opportunity in your business.

Then, to ensure that he can realize the opportunity he will very carefully assess the risk.

The buyer's point of view can be expressed with a simple equation:

$$\text{Buyer Value} = \frac{\text{Benefit (Stable, sustainable and improving revenues, margins, cash flow and profits)}}{\text{Risk (Reduction of financial, operational, business, market, economic risks)}}$$

In my years of representing entrepreneurs, there have been only a handful of times that I've met one who actually understands the buyer's mindset.

The buyer, at the very core, is an investor looking for a rate of return on their investment. In doing so, they must not overpay relative to the underlying opportunity and minimize their risk.

A buyer may pay extra depending on his cost of capital. The lower the cost of capital, the more flexibility the buyer has to pay a higher multiple to get the deal done.

The buyer graphic shows what the buyer wants and some of the variables involved in his expectation of a target return on investment (ROI):

Once you start viewing the buyer as an investor who is really buying an opportunity, you can put on your entrepreneurial hat and start positioning your business as that opportunity in order to get maximum sale price.

This is where the seller and the buyer dance will begin. The seller will upsell every aspect of the business, downplay risk and paint a rosy picture of the future.

The buyer, on the other hand, will make a case for a lower purchase price due to risks, errors, inefficiencies, deficiencies and liabilities.

How Buyers View Acquisition Opportunities

The buyer has an entirely different view of how he or she needs to purchase and has a methodology for going about it.

For starters, from day one you've focused on cash.

Most advisors will tell you that's the thing to do. Get your revenues up. Get your margins up. Improve your cash flow. Increase your profits.

I agree 100% with this advice. I tell my clients the same things.

Just remember that your revenues, margins, cash flow and profits are table stakes to get into the game. Those are the prerequisites to the sale. The buyer is looking beyond those.

In fact, he's likely looking at a whole bunch of companies and will weed out the ones that don't fit his criteria. When I'm working on the buy side, the client and I will sit down and talk about what he is trying to accomplish.

He will tell me something like "I want a company that is

between $20-50 million in revenue, with an EBITDA of at least 20%." The company will also have to be in a certain geographic territory. It needs to be growing at least 15% a year with a strong competitive position in the market, etc.

When my team and I search for these companies, we may identify hundreds of targets, which we boil down to the top 20, the top 10, top 5 and then the top 3 through our process of vetting.

By the time the client starts talking to the top candidates, the revenues and the profits are simply prerequisites to the discussion. While revenue, margins and cash flow are important factors; a lot of other variables will ultimately decide which company the client acquires.

The next graphic shows how a strategic buyer will generally look at a transaction. Beyond being a cultural fit, the buyer will look at industry growth, target company position, capital expenditures, working capital needs, cost of capital, synergies, integration elements etc. to come up with a valuation and/or purchase valuation.

How a Strategic Buyer Looks at an Acquisition

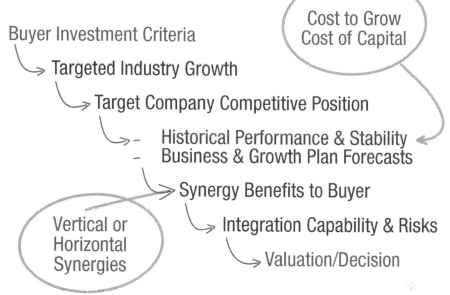

Buyer Investment Criteria

↳ Targeted Industry Growth

   ↳ Target Company Competitive Position

     ↳ Historical Performance & Stability
        Business & Growth Plan Forecasts

       ↳ Synergy Benefits to Buyer

        ↳ Integration Capability & Risks

         ↳ Valuation/Decision

Cost to Grow Cost of Capital

Vertical or Horizontal Synergies

What you need to remember is that just because a buyer wants to enter into a letter of intent to purchase your company that doesn't mean the deal will get done. There are loads of variables involved in his decision and he's most likely negotiating multiple letters of intent.

The buyer's eventual investment decision will be based on the balance between the potential opportunities and risks within your company and how these opportunities and risks are likely to affect an acceptable return on investment.

Preparing
Your Business
for Sale

Chapter 15.

When to Start Getting Ready

Many entrepreneurs are often unaware they need a realistic time frame to enhance the value of their business so that it can be sold for the greatest payout possible.

Worse, most haven't aligned their retirement cash needs with a realistic valuation of the business they hope to sell.

That can have a huge impact on their retirement plans. There is danger of tremendous retirement shortfalls and financial gaps.

All because of poor planning.

If you are as smart as I believe you are, then you will take my next point to heart.

I don't care how good of an advisor you hire to help you sell your company, you will likely end up leaving a big pile of money on the table.

By the time you're ready to sell, it's almost always too late. You should have started planning years ago.

Take a look at the following graphic. You'll see there are three stages to maximizing exit value. Most entrepreneurs are focused on "price" with little regard to anything else. You just skipped over stage #1 entirely – and that is where the money is.

Maximizing Exit Value

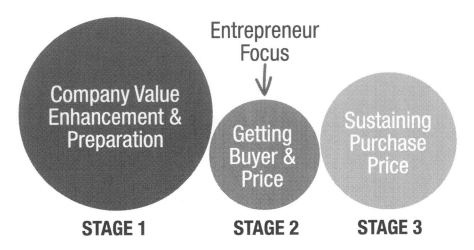

But if you start early enough and focus on substantially improving your business's valuation, you can potentially double or triple its valuation.

Maybe you can do even better.

By starting early enough, I mean years before you plan to exit.

The ideal time frame to harvest maximum valuation for a company is to begin the process 3-5 years prior to exit.

The Exit Horizons graphic lays out the suggested timeline:

Exit Horizons
Prior to Sale

Sale **4** 3-12 months
Find Buyers
& Close

3 0-12 months
Clean Up

2 1-3 years
Increase
Value

1 3-5 years
Lay the
Foundation

If you want to sell your business at a premium price, you will likely need to implement various initiatives within your company to improve performance and mitigate risk. All of this generally requires significant time, patience and effort. It is best to start years prior to the exit. Besides, trying to put lipstick on a pig when you're at the closing table is not a good strategy.

Chapter 16.

Reverse Due Diligence

Most entrepreneurs have up to 80% of their net worth in their businesses. The problem is that businesses are generally illiquid assets. If your overall net worth is $10,000,000 and the company is about $8,000,000 of that number, this can have serious consequences if you don't unlock and liquidate its value properly.

Naturally, doing that requires some preparation. And this is where the problem is.

Most entrepreneurs don't realize that they need to prepare their businesses for their exit. When they decide to sell, most just call a business broker or M&A adviser and list their business for sale. They think it is just that simple. They couldn't be more wrong.

Look at it this way: If you were selling your house, you'd probably want to do a little painting, maybe change the carpets and fix that broken gutter. You'd want to gussy things up a bit before you planted that "For Sale" sign on the front lawn. It's the same with a business. Yet failure to properly prepare is the most common mistake most sellers – especially entrepreneurs – make.

Not only do most entrepreneurs fail to prepare, they don't have a clear idea of what they need to do and the time it will take to do it. Investing preparation time and resources in your biggest asset – your business – can make a huge difference in your net worth. I worked with a client whose company had an initial valuation of $28 million. Twenty-eight months of clean up, preparation, enhancement and posturing later, the company was sold for more than $60 million.

In order to get your company prepared, a reverse due diligence exercise needs to be conducted in advance of listing the business for sale. This will involve cleaning up existing operations, fixing blemishes, addressing financial disparities and otherwise rectifying situations that might lead to a lower value.

During your reverse due diligence, you will spot changes that would improve, optimize, clean up and better organize the company. These should be prioritized based on impact on exit value, available resources and time frame to exit, and then undertaken in proper order.

This graphic illustrates the normal due diligence process I use with my clients:

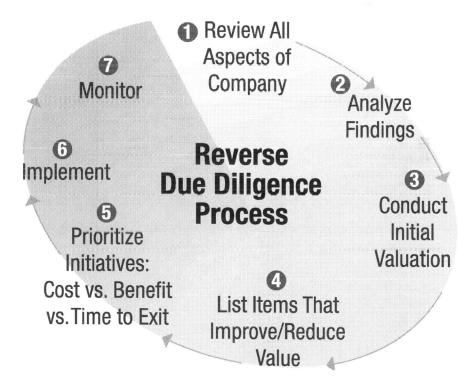

In the reverse due diligence process, I create a virtual cloud-based data room for my clients and organize data based on a hierarchy.

It is advisable to time stamp the materials and keep them updated to maintain a state of readiness. Once you've created a virtual data room and an effective hierarchy, it would not take that much time to continually update that data room and keep it current.

One of the first things that needs to happen as a part of the reverse due diligence exercise is to get a realistic idea of what your business is actually worth.

Once you know the value, this will set the stage for what could improve or reduce your company value – taking into account your exit timeline and your available resources.

Begin by sitting down with your management team and advisors to lay out a clear path to exit. Make sure that you stay realistic.

I put my clients through a process that involves getting all stakeholders focused on how we move forward to maximize exit value within the requisite timeline.

Step back and take a hard, unbiased look at your company. Imagine you have never seen your company before and try to see it through the lens of a stranger. This is easier said than done because often we are so close to our own businesses that we lose objectivity. So, don't try to go it alone.

Getting Stakeholders Focused

❶ Get a Baseline Valuation

❷ Lay Out a Clear Strategy to Increase Value

❸ Lay Out a Realistic Operations Plan

❻ Align Planning with Entrepreneur's Exit Plan

❺ Get Realistic on Financial Assumptions & Available Resources

❹ Break Plan into Clear Action Items

An experienced advisor working closely with you and other stakeholders will help you stay objective and focused on implementing the right initiatives to improve sale valuation.

Chapter 17.

People Issues

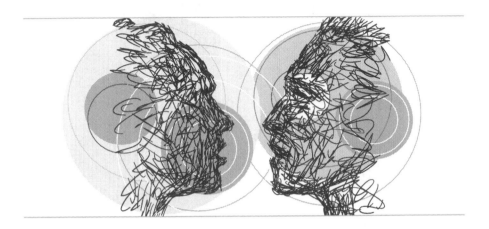

Let's put these into two separate categories:

1. Employees and Management

2. Shareholders and Stakeholders

Employees and Management

For most of us, people are our biggest asset, yet we never really view them as such. We view them as human beings. We call them John, Jack, Jane. Many of us entrepreneurs are very concerned about our employees. We feel tremendous loyalty to them. Larger companies tend to do a better job at seeing employees as assets.

But we really don't make that connection. As a result, when I am working with a company on a value enhancement engagement, I commonly find all kinds of personnel related issues.

Common Personnel Related Issues

- Talent Gaps
- Ineffective Job Descriptions
- Outdated Training
- Lack of Incentive Compensation
- Minimal Accountabilities
- No Intellectual Property Assignment Agreements
- Non-Existent Employment Agreements

Some of this happens because we are busy pulling out fires or have knowledge gaps or lack of resources. In addition to that, we're not looking at our employees as a valuable human capital asset that can help us increase not just our profits but also our exit value.

Excluding the entrepreneur, every business has one, two or a handful of key employees that are essential to the organization being able to sustain and grow its revenues, profits and cash flow.

If you agree with me that these key employees are one of your biggest assets and if your asset goes to lunch and simply decides to never come back, what is the net impact to your business? What if this happens a month before your very carefully planned exit?

If we really took on an asset-oriented mindset, we would

secure our assets. We would ensure that we had proper contracts with our employees, especially the key ones, in a manner that secures them to the business and keeps them performing before the exit, during the exit and after the exit to fulfill your post-closing obligations and maximize the potential of your earn-out, if applicable.

On the other hand, many of our employees are not assets. They're actually liabilities – for multiple reasons. Maybe they're non-performers, overpaid, under-utilized, lazy or just plain incompetent.

Many of these employees would be the first to go if your company was to be acquired. Remember, your buyer is an investor buying as asset. They are not emotional. If you have employees that are overpaid or non-performing and are not helping you move the needle, they're essentially sucking up your cash.

People = Cash

Even though this might not be a task you'll relish, you must take action and optimize the work force long before the exit. If you don't, you just handed a sizeable gift to the buyer.

Let's assume that a company pays $140,000 in payroll for employees that fit in this category.

$140,000 X Multiple of 6= **$840,000**

This $840,000 is your gift to the buyer. Your inaction can cost you a lot of money. The reality is that if you don't do it, the buyer most definitely will.

Caveat: Please consult an employment attorney and take necessary steps to minimize headaches.

Take this example: One of my client companies employed

an executive assistant. Jane had been with the company for 20 plus years. She was the CEO's right-hand person and both of them felt a significant affinity for each other. Jane started at an annual salary of $30,000 but in the year the company was sold, she was making $87,000 while her job replacement value in the market was about $45,000.

Prior to sale, my client and I talked about Jane. He mentioned that she had talked about retiring a year or so prior, however he was uncomfortable having a conversation with her. When the company was acquired, Jane was among those employees that the buyer chose not to employ. Not only was Jane out of a job, it cost my client a pretty penny. In this case, the business was sold at 7x its earnings.

My client's inaction cost him Jane's replacement cost differential (salary and benefits) $50,000 x 7 = $350,000 in additional sale value. He could have easily cut Jane a $150,000 check to aid toward retirement and still would have come out ahead. Not only did Jane walk away with a fraction of that, my client successfully ended up hurting himself as well.

Buyers are very smart. They will feast on your inefficiencies. Many of these inefficiencies are a direct cash gift from you to them and serve as an excellent purchase price subsidy to the buyer.

My suggestion is optimize your work force, clean house. Get the right people on the ship. Get the wrong people off the ship. Make sure your people are not dramatically overpaid unless they are valuable key employees that are important to the business. By the way, even if the buyer says they will not get rid of your employees, after some time operating the business, they will realize inefficiencies and make the tough decisions.

Shareholders and Stakeholders

It is imperative that all stakeholders and shareholders including, but not limited to, your partners, investors, successors, key employees, managers, family members (if applicable) and advisors are made aware of what you are about to do. Everybody needs to be on the same page on these:

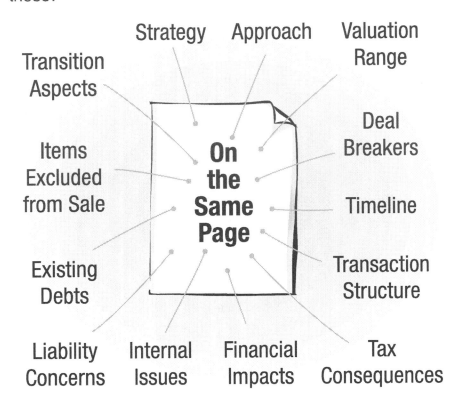

You do not want a lot of second-guessing behind your back and/or people working against you because they simply do not agree with your exit approach.

Various types of disputes, disagreements and conflicts can materialize en route to an exit. Keep in mind that even when you have shared your plans with your stakeholders, nothing is written in stone. An exit can be a fluid situation. People can change their minds and all kinds of unexpected surprises can pop up on all kinds of matters – the type of consideration offered, biases towards potential acquirers, disagreements over the future company direction and terms of the deal. So, keep the lines of communication open.

If you previously raised external funds from venture capitalists or other professional investors, there are likely protective provisions in their agreements with you that may prohibit you from selling the business, so consult your investors early. Your idea of company valuation and timeline may be very different than your investors'.

Valuation disagreements can quickly turn minority shareholders into hostile minority shareholders. While the minority shares are indeed a minority, shareholder litigation can be a detriment to a deal. Buyers don't want to step into a hornets' nest. Resolve your issues before you go to market to sell your business.

In order to reduce headaches and/or improve value, it is imperative that you open up lines of communication with all key parties and optimize your work force.

Aligning key exit variables with shareholders and other stakeholders prior to starting the sale process will pay significant dividends. At a minimum, it will minimize meddling, second-guessing and disagreements during the transaction.

Your key employees are vital assets (and in some cases liabilities) when it comes to selling your company. You must ensure an optimal work force with the right short-term and long-term incentives in place to keep your employees performing before, during and after the sale.

Chapter 18.

Financial Issues

Would you buy a house if you couldn't do an inspection? Would you buy it if you couldn't verify where the property line was? Would you buy a house if you thought it had termite issues but the seller wouldn't let you inside to confirm your suspicions?

I wouldn't and I'll bet neither would you. Such is the case with the financials of a business. Many entrepreneurs run lifestyle businesses. Our businesses are an extension of ourselves and we run them the way we see fit. Some of us run them really cleanly. Some of us run them the other way.

One of the biggest value destructors is the lack of financial transparency. This occurs for various reasons. However, if the buyer cannot trust the quality of your financials, the purchase price undoubtedly will go down. If the buyer does not walk away from the onset, at the very minimum, it will increase due diligence time and costs (costs that you are paying – NOT the buyer).

There could be a plethora of reasons that raise doubts about the quality of financial information within a company. Among them:

Inaccurate Records

Unavailable Records

Obsolete Assets

Common Financial Issues

Unreconciled Accounts

Lifestyle Expenses

Unreported Cash

Improper Revenue Recognition

Comingled Expenses

Entrepreneurs can have a strong focus on reducing taxes. Some of us can be in the "expense" rather than "capitalize" mindset. Not only are we running personal lifestyle expenses through the business, we don't track what we ran through or when. Often, we forget what these expenses are. A lot of our finances are comingled. As a result, we don't really have an idea of what our true profitability is.

In addition, our balance sheets often have assets (such as real estate) that are severely undervalued. In other cases, assets are overvalued or simply don't belong on the balance sheet. Since we don't manage our financials properly, we may have many unfunded or underfunded off balance sheet liabilities that can materialize in the form of purchase price adjustments, clawbacks or litigation.

So what needs to happen?

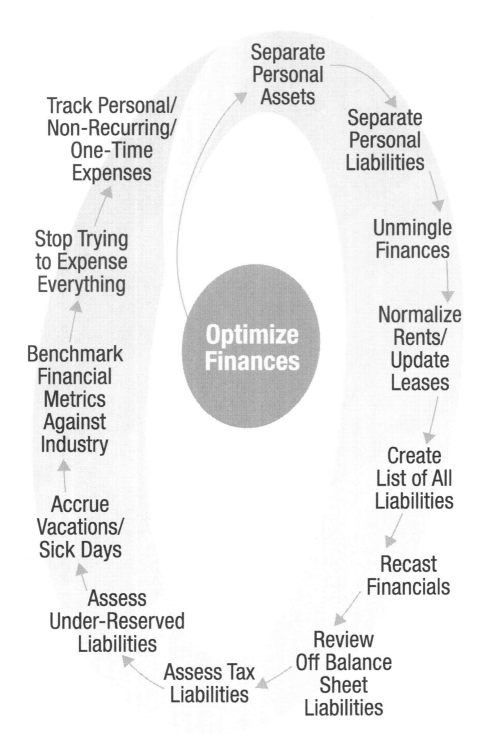

Separate Personal Assets

Track Personal/ Non-Recurring/ One-Time Expenses

Separate Personal Liabilities

Stop Trying to Expense Everything

Unmingle Finances

Benchmark Financial Metrics Against Industry

Optimize Finances

Normalize Rents/ Update Leases

Accrue Vacations/ Sick Days

Create List of All Liabilities

Assess Under-Reserved Liabilities

Recast Financials

Assess Tax Liabilities

Review Off Balance Sheet Liabilities

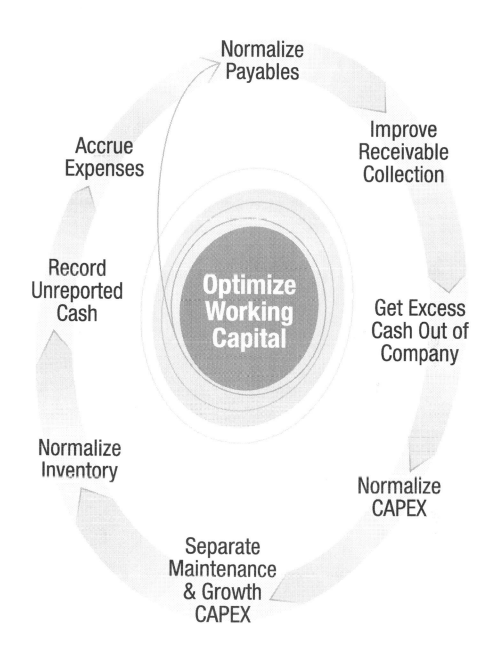

It is imperative that you clean house and run your financials cleanly. Failure to do so will severely cripple your exit value or wreak nasty surprises that could have been avoided.

Besides the quality of your financials, how you perform financially is mission critical. One disconnect I often see with entrepreneurs is that while they know that good performance is desirable, they may not realize how much a positive revenue trend line over a multiple year period really impacts their exit valuation.

When I look over an entrepreneur's books in my M&A Advisor role, I often see inconsistent revenues and margins. Buyers do not like feast or famine revenues and margins. By that, I mean you have great revenues one year and the next your revenues are horrible. Declining revenues and margin trends are not helpful, either. Flat revenue growth is not good and declining order backlogs are value reducers.

Here are a few things to remember:

Escalating revenues, margins and cash flow reduce risk. Stability and history of performance provide peace of mind to the buyer because he is using your financial performance and cash flows to finance the transaction.

No buyer will be interested in purchasing your company without understanding all the assets and liabilities – on and off the balance sheet – he or she will be taking on.

If your financials can't be trusted, the buyer will likely walk away or demand a substantial discount and/or onerous terms to justify the risk of unknowns.

Financial transparency is mission critical to achieving a valuation that you can live with or be excited about. So, take the time, put in the effort and get your company finances in order long before you decide to sell.

Chapter 19.

Sales and Marketing Issues

Of course your market position is important to you. It's also important to the buyer. In fact, the better your market position, generally the higher the multiple.

Buyers like momentum and they hate the loss thereof. They are buying opportunity and, naturally, they want some reasonable assurances that your company will continue to perform.

They will make sure that you have vetted your sales and marketing methods, refined the processes and have an effective return on marketing dollars spent.

You will be rewarded for a strong brand identity and penalized for a weak one. If you are in a market that's growing slowly, your valuation will be affected.

If you have a poor distribution channel, your value will also take a hit. A strong sales team, effective training, robust databases, sound practices, visibility into your sales metrics and a strong sales pipeline will generally drive your valuation to the higher end of your range.

Lack of effective marketing tactics, confused strategies, ineffective tracking metrics, failed campaigns, no return on investment on the marketing spend, long and dismal sales cycles and limited brand identity all lead to a destruction of value.

Here's what needs to happen:

Marketing and sales are the core drivers of every successful company's lifeblood: Revenues. If you haven't sold your products and services in steadily increasing volumes over the past few years, it will likely hurt your valuation. In order to maximize your exit valuation, be prepared to show that the entire spectrum of your marketing and sales effort is well organized and well managed.

Chapter 20.
Operational Issues

Operational issues come in all shapes and sizes. They could be the result of a leadership problem, infrastructure of the company, inefficient internal controls or a host of other issues. Instead of boring you with dozens of pages related to operations, I'll bore you with a visual view of what an entrepreneur should be doing to optimize operations.

Performance

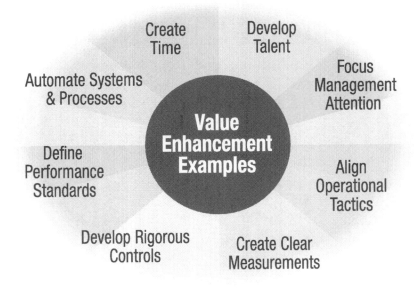

Create Time

Develop Talent

Automate Systems & Processes

Focus Management Attention

Value Enhancement Examples

Define Performance Standards

Align Operational Tactics

Develop Rigorous Controls

Create Clear Measurements

Operations

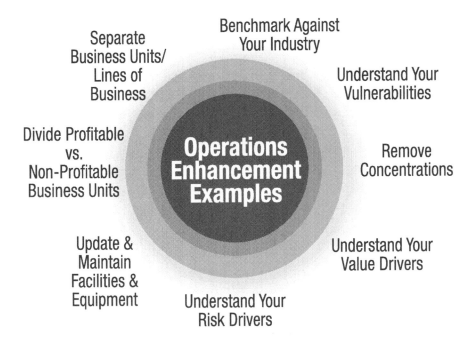

Separate Business Units/ Lines of Business

Benchmark Against Your Industry

Understand Your Vulnerabilities

Divide Profitable vs. Non-Profitable Business Units

Operations Enhancement Examples

Remove Concentrations

Update & Maintain Facilities & Equipment

Understand Your Value Drivers

Understand Your Risk Drivers

Production & Inventory

Assess Inventory

Remove Inventory Bloat

Improve Production Scheduling & Throughput

Remove Obsolete Inventory

Assess Production Procedures & Protocols

Production & Inventory Enhancement Examples

Minimize Bad Forecasting

Improve Order-to-Delivery Cycle Times

Improve Purchasing Controls

Remove Production Bottlenecks

Operational inefficiencies suck up working capital and reduce cash flow, margins and profitability. This impacts the exit valuation from the onset and sometimes can serve as a purchase price subsidy to the buyer. In many cases, opportunistic buyers leverage these operational issues further during the "purchase cycle" to reduce the agreed upon purchase price to the detriment of the entrepreneur.

Chapter 21.

Legal Issues

If you don't already have one, get a decent attorney and have him or her conduct a thorough legal audit.

Make sure all your leases are current with decent residual periods and, ideally, with some reasonable termination options. Remember, a buyer's operating strategy may be entirely different from yours. Your lease can quickly become a liability.

If you own a restaurant in a great location, you would want to ensure that there's a fair amount of time left on the lease as well as reasonable renewal options. On the other hand, if you're a manufacturer, the buyer may consolidate your operations into his and may not want to assume the lease of your facility. Thus leaving you holding the bag on your lease.

If you have a lot of handshake customers, you need to get them under contract, if at all possible. In some industries, it's not feasible to have customer contracts because customers operate from purchase order to purchase order. To the extent that you can, have written contracts with your customers. If you've got non-assignable customer contracts, you need to know about those so you can disclose to the buyer before negotiations begin.

Be sure to:

Get Employment Agreements

Think Through 3rd Party Clearance Issues

Get Intellectual Property Agreements

Do a Lien Search on Your Company

Examples: Legal Considerations

Ensure There Are No Missing Contracts

Settle Disputes, Lawsuits & Claims

Get Contracts with Handshake Customers

Revisit Licensing Agreements

Update Leases

Being prepared legally is paramount to being able to sell your business. Think of it as a proactive exercise. I like to think of it as "Sleep Insurance." It allows you to minimize unnecessary headaches mid-transaction and provide peace of mind. Do you really want to find out that you have liens against your company or are missing a key licensing agreement at the closing table? Either of which may significantly delay or derail your exit.

Chapter 22.

Intellectual Property

Entrepreneurs don't put enough emphasis on intellectual property and how it can reduce risk and protect revenue.

Ensure that patents, trademarks and copyrights are filed correctly. If you have existing patents, determine the residual life of each. Often, in the case of patents, entrepreneurs file too soon and don't get the right coverage, and there's little or no focus on international expansion and global patent standards.

Even though you may never intend to expand internationally, that doesn't mean that your acquirer won't. When dealing with important assets like patents, you need to make sure that you are using the right attorney who will focus on global patent standards.

Review your intellectual property title chain to ensure that there is a clear title to your intellectual property. Often entrepreneurs use multiple providers externally and may not have a clear title. Ensure that you have work-for-hire agreements with all your contractors.

Often, intellectual property is owned by the entrepreneur personally and is not assigned to the company. This can create problems at the last minute. In some cases, there is exposure to claims from previous employers because the entrepreneur was working for someone else at the time and has created a derivative work using the previous employer's intellectual property.

Most entrepreneurs have no centralized strategy for the collection, documentation and protection of intellectual property. This leads to all kinds of issues like missing source code, ineffective version controls of source code and improper standardization.

Here's what you need to do to leverage your intellectual property to increase exit value:

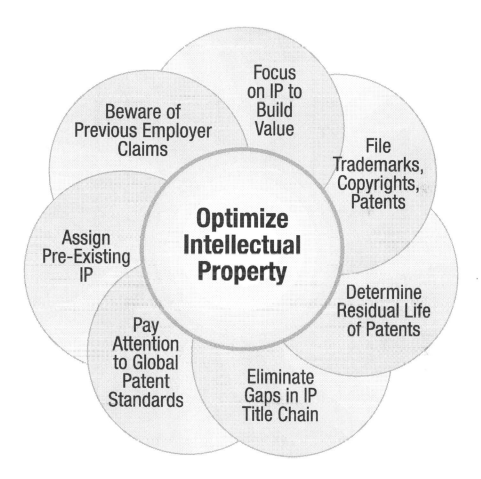

If you want to sell your company for more than its cash flow, you need to pay careful attention to the many intangible assets that don't appear on your balance sheet.

In the following diagram you can see examples of some of these intangibles:

Leverage Intangible Assets

Systems, Methodologies, Specialized Know-How, Proprietary Technology

Rituals & Activities that Sustain Performance Within Your Culture

Collective Intellectual Capital of Employees

Scale: Number of Locations, Geographic Diversity, Distribution Channels

Market Position, Momentum

Propreitary Databases, Difficult to Get Permits, Gov't/Municipal Contracts

Brand, Reputation, Logo, Trademarks, Patents, Copyrights

Operational Tactics, Performance Standards, Quality Control Procedures

You'll want to highlight your intangibles when dealing with buyers because they are the reasons why the buyer would pay above market pricing and will go a long way in helping you be in the top end of the valuation range for your industry.

Start by making out a complete list of your important intellectual property. I am not just talking about patents but also trademarks, copyrights, proprietary know-how or methodologies, trade secrets, technology, key systems and more.

It is imperative that the potential buyer fully understands the value of these invisible assets and how they can be leveraged to create competitive advantage, grow revenues and sustain margins.

Chapter 23.

Lack of Barriers to Entry

Many times, entrepreneurs don't understand what barriers to entry are. They can range from software and specialized processes to licenses and trade secrets.

Strong barriers to entry can keep competitors from moving in on your turf – and enhance company valuation at exit time.

Buyers look at barriers to entry as key elements of risk reduction when assessing companies. If you have proprietary intellectual property, this may represent a competitive advantage that can protect, sustain and grow your market position.

This reduces buyer risk and will generally help improve exit valuation. Barriers to entry can be of all kinds.

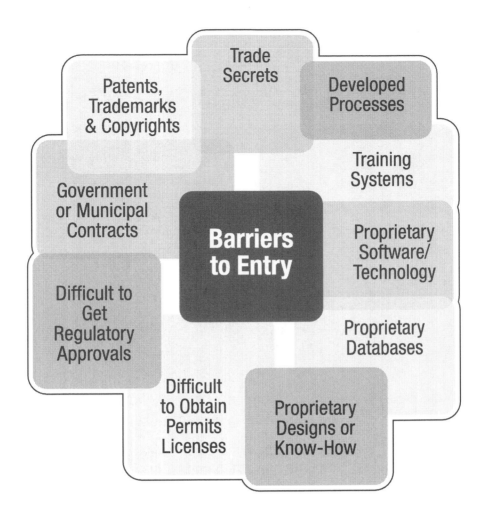

Barriers to entry are traditionally used to build defenses to keep your competitors from entering your market, but they can also be instrumental in improving cost economies.

A company could get key suppliers to agree to long-term contracts with preferential pricing and/or lock up raw material supply in the market, giving that company a major leg up on competitors.

In many cases, barriers to entry could substantially increase company revenues. A unique, hard to replicate business model is a good example of that.

Think hard about everything that gives you an advantage over current or potential competitors. Do you have proprietary technology, unique manufacturing processes, hard to get licenses? Understand, document and be prepared to clearly articulate these barriers to entry. The last thing a potential buyer wants to do is buy your company knowing that one or more new competitors could appear at any time.

Here is a rule of thumb with barriers to entry: The harder it is for new competitors to enter your company's target market(s), the more attractive your company will be to potential buyers, resulting in a higher likelihood of a premium exit valuation.

Chapter 24.

Dealing With Concentrations

Early on, the buyer will focus on various types of concentrations within your company. These concentrations can range from industry to products, customers, suppliers and employees.

Customer Concentration

If more than 10% of your revenue comes from one customer, you may have a customer concentration problem. In this type of scenario, the buyer will either walk away or demand a significant purchase price discount and/or onerous terms because this significantly increases the buyer's risk.

For example, the buyer may try to shift a significant amount of risk to you by demanding that you provide significant seller financing, take a large portion of the purchase price in an earn-out or demand that a significant amount of the purchase price is placed in an escrow for an extended period of time.

If you have an existing customer concentration problem and you have time, diversify your revenue. If you don't, it will cost you an arm and a leg. If the customer concentration is unavoidable, then there are two things you should do:

1. You must disclose the customer concentration problem

long before you ever start negotiating. This will save time and improve your negotiating leverage. There's no reason to go down a path with a buyer without disclosing this upfront. It will save you time, hassle and money.

2. Do a financial analysis of what would happen if your large customer fired you. Remember, large customers use large resources, employees and space in your facility – not to mention equipment, materials, inventory etc. Calculate the true financial impact encompassing both revenue and expenses. Buyers tend to focus on the revenue side and often don't stick around to look at the expense side.

I have seen situations where after this analysis was done, the net impact to profits was neutral or minimal. You have to be proactive and get ahead of this major issue. The key is that you have to prepare in advance and be ready to provide net impact analysis to the buyer by simulating a large customer loss.

Supplier Concentration

Hard-to-replace suppliers can add significant operating risk to a company. If you have a supplier concentration because you have a hard-to-replace supplier who makes highly specialized products and/or provides proprietary services for you, you need to ensure that you have a long-term contract in place with that supplier.

That said; don't blindly sign away a long-term binding agreement. Your business strategy may change and your buyer's business strategy may be entirely different from yours. You want to make sure there's some flexibility built into terminating the contract from your end.

Key Employee Concentrations

Besides owner concentrations where the business relies too heavily on the owner, key employee concentrations can be equally detrimental. Often I find that the business depends on one or two key employees who are mission critical to the business. Should they die, get disabled or depart, the company revenues can be significantly hurt.

You need to ensure that these people are locked down in a strong contract so they can perform before, during and after the sale enabling you to harvest maximum value. Often I advise clients to set up a sinking fund with a vesting schedule that incentivizes employees to stick around. You can also add a portion of the sale proceeds to the sinking fund to improve results.

What you don't want is to get a call from your buyer, long after you have closed, telling you that two of your key employees have left and you will most likely not collect your earn-out or other contingent payment, costing you millions. That will not make for a fun day.

We all know it is rarely a good idea to put all your eggs in one basket. Similarly, a business that relies too heavily on one customer, one supplier, a key employee or even one product or service can be seen as a risky investment by a potential buyer. Still, not all concentrations are perceived as high risk. If you are in a niche business or have a unique specialization, this may actually work to your company's – and your potential buyer's – advantage.

Chapter 25.

The Human Factor

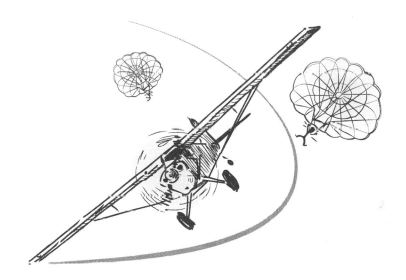

Buyers don't like to buy companies that can't operate without their owners. If they don't walk away from the deal, they want significant concessions. They will make certain that the purchase price and the underlying terms are aggressively favorable to them.

If your business relies heavily on you and you don't have the time and inclination to find a fix, expect to discuss significant accommodations like seller notes, earn-outs and other types of contingent and/or deferred payments.

Heavy reliance on the owner is among the biggest value destructors to a business.

Now, there is a difference between being self-employed

and being an entrepreneur. If you are self-employed, one day you will shut your business down, and if you have been wise, you've saved enough to see you through retirement.

If you are an entrepreneur you have likely operated your business with more financial exposures. You have made capital improvements, signed personal guarantees and invested money in growth initiatives. Your business has sucked up a lot of your savings and operating cash.

Consciously or sub-consciously many of us have an expectation that we will one day sell our business and use those proceeds in the next chapter of our lives. However, because we are so tactical and the company relies so heavily on us, the value of the business is severely diminished.

I tell my clients that once your company gets to be a certain size and you've got some functional managers and a decent team in place, it's time for you to manage your business strategically and get out of tactical operations of the business. It is time to find a successor.

Here's why I say that:

1. I want the business to be able to operate without you.

2. You are the leader. And I would like for you to be 100% focused on the strategic and high value activities that increase value rather than on tactical items that can be managed by a subordinate.

"Internally transitioning to a successor" is a tall order and can be akin to bailing out of a jet at 30,000 feet while your successor is simultaneously parachuting in to take your place. Not an easy task. There will be plenty of turbulence.

Here is what needs to happen:

Entrepreneur Succession

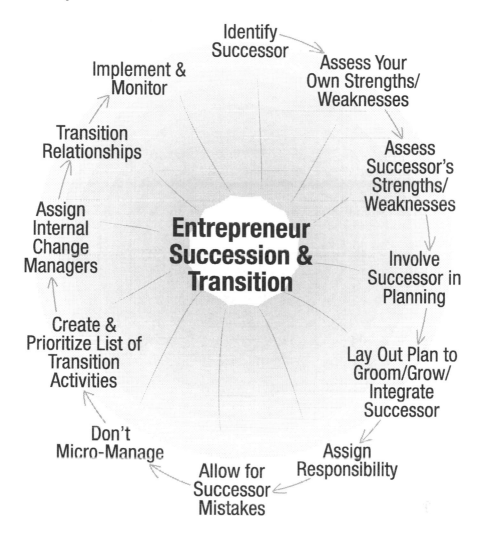

If you haven't identified and trained your successor, it is highly unlikely the company will succeed if you leave for any reason.

The reality is that if you can't show the potential buyer that you have the right team in place to ensure that the business will succeed and continue to grow without you, this will likely impact the purchase price and/or the underlying terms.

To seriously maximize value, I would be tickled pink if you fired yourself. In an ideal situation, it would be perfect if you played a lot of golf or traveled a lot and rarely came into the office. You'd have a great team in place so you could manage the company at the board level. All while the revenues, margins, cash flow and profits were in a positive trend line.

Like a buddy of mine says, "The true job of leader is to work himself out of a job."

Need Help?

Visit www.ExitBomb.Org/Programs and create an Exit Program to help you clean up, enhance value and subsequently, exit your company for maximum value. Programs are available for external exits (third-party sale), internal transitions (transfer to family or sale to employees) and even "No Exit Exits" (maintain ownership with no active involvement). All programs are guided by Exit Bomb advisors, tailored to your exit timeline and can range from a few months to a few years.

Preparing Yourself
for the Exit

Chapter 26.

Planning Your Exit

Of all the investments you make in your business, exit planning just may provide the biggest return.

Then again, I can't prove that. There isn't a ton of available research that compares the benefits of exit planning vs. the benefits of doing nothing.

I've got a theory about why that is. There aren't any benefits to not creating an exit plan. It's very difficult to compare something that exists with something that doesn't.

According to a survey, 75% of business owners have not done any exit planning at all.[3] We're so busy putting out fires and dealing with the day-to-day stuff that there's little time left for planning. Especially planning for an exit.

It's a sad fact but:

Many business owners will spend more time planning a family vacation to the Grand Canyon than they will planning their exit.

Business owners who actually create a plan tend to be more in control. They choose when they want to exit and they do so on their terms and timeline.

---

3 Exit Planning Institute

Benefits of Exit Planning

An exit plan is a strategic roadmap that allows the entrepreneur to successfully exit the business on their terms and their timeline for maximum value with the least amount of taxes while aligning personal, family and financial goals with business goals.

Helping you create such a plan is why I wrote this book. An exit plan deals with all kinds of issues:

Don't confuse exit planning with estate planning. Estate planning is all about the minimization of estate taxes and personal bequests made by the individual in relation to their estate.

Exit planning is a collaborative process and involves the creation of a team of key advisors and stakeholders to lay out a strategic and tactical roadmap that fits your unique and specific circumstances.

You don't enter the New Year without a plan for the next 12 months. You don't go into a meeting with a big new customer or your investor without preparation. Unless you are very lucky, exiting your company without a plan is a recipe for disaster.

The time to do exit planning is many years prior to the business being sold. The task of aligning personal, family and financial goals with business goals requires careful coordination and focus. It is best to start this process early on. Separate initiatives need to be taken to get you mentally prepared and ready – along with the alignment of your personal finances with your business.

Chapter 27.

Alignment With Your Finances

When I talk to my M&A clients about alignment, I usually hear, "Alignment? What do I need to align with?"

I tell them that, for starters, the bulk of his or her net worth is most likely in the business. In industry speak we call this a "net worth concentration." If this is the case, then that's where the money for retirement or the next step will come from.

Let me help connect the dots further.

There are four types of alignment gaps:

1. Financial

2. Estate Planning

3. Family

4. Life After the Exit

Let's take them one at a time.

Financial

I have seen multiple surveys highlighting that more than half of entrepreneurs don't know what their companies are worth. Many don't know how much money they need to retire. And most haven't taken the time to look at their existing resources vs. how much money they need to retire and what their business valuation/sale can actually provide them.

They are operating with real risk that they could have significant retirement shortfalls. In fact, six out of ten business owners will delay retirement with many citing financial reasons.[4]

Many business owners comingle their personal finances with the business. Part of this is because that's where the cash is. The other part is that they can run personal expenses through the company for tax reasons. Business owners don't calculate the value of these personal expenses. After the exit event, they come to a realization that replacing some of these still continuing expenses further adds to their financial shortfall.

Because of comingling and, in many cases, lax tracking and controls, the company financials can be in disarray. Many entrepreneurs do not know the true profitability of their business because of the lifestyle impact I've just described.

They often have a tax deduction mindset where they are running expenses through a company. Their focus is to reduce taxes. As a result, the entrepreneur/owner may not be aware of the true profitability of the business. This can keep the owner in the business longer than they want to be.

Your business tax returns are separate, right? True. But the tax impact is generally borne by the entrepreneur. Your choice of entity structure also impacts your spouse. You know the house she wants to build when you bring home the big bacon? Good luck pal! Your entity structure can take the mansion to a shack in an instant.

---

4 Gallup Poll

If you are a C-corporation, depending on your transaction structure, you may be subject to double tax and, depending on the state you live in, the tax bite could be 60% plus. Yikes!!! My point is that owners do not optimize their tax position prior to sale. In many cases, they don't realize the heavy tax implications until it's too late.

Do you really want a tax awakening after you've signed on the dotted line?

Estate Planning

Often owners have an opportunity that they don't harvest in estate planning, gifting, asset protection and charitable bequests. Needless to say, life and financial stage will dictate how seriously you look at some of these planning opportunities. My point is, since your business is likely one of the biggest assets in your overall portfolio, it would be wise to have a macro view of things.

Remember, a business sale creates cash. This cash creates taxes. Your remaining cash is subject to claim should you get sued personally for something you did, advertently or inadvertently.

If you are like most people, when you reach a certain age, you may become more conservative and consume less, and will be more concerned with potentially outliving your income. Money tends to grow, especially if you have some time for it to do that, even if you have invested it conservatively.

When death occurs, your residual estate may create estate taxes. Haven't you paid enough taxes along the way? Need I go on?

When planning to exit your business, align your business (which is an asset) with your other assets and other financial and personal goals. You would be surprised to see how many otherwise smart entrepreneurs keep their personal and business planning separate. This is a serious oversight.

Family

If you have family members in the business, make sure they are on the same page.

In other words, make sure you take their concerns into consideration. Align your family priorities with the business as well. Family business dynamics are terribly complex. Often there is tremendous disagreement between the children, internal politics and other family issues. The entrepreneur often deals with all kinds of personal issues in addition to running a business.

The spouse may be resentful because not all of the children were treated equally. Many of the family members that were outside the business may be resentful of the financial treatment of family members who were active in the business.

Life After the Exit

Entrepreneurs can often have a serious loss of personal fulfillment resulting from a loss of business relationships. One day you are king of the hill dealing with your customers, suppliers, employees and business colleagues. The next day you are facing different realities.

It is imperative that you figure out what you will do post-exit – before you exit.

The key element to keep in mind here is that it is critical to align your personal finances, tax implications and personal and family priorities with your business; align with what is most likely the single biggest asset in your net worth.

Chapter 28.

Timing Your Exit

The timing of when to exit your business is extremely important yet incredibly complex. There are several factors beyond your earnings that can impact exit value:

Your Age

I hate to bring this up, but it's a fact we all have to deal with: The older you get, generally, the lower the value of your business.

Why?

Timing Factors – Age

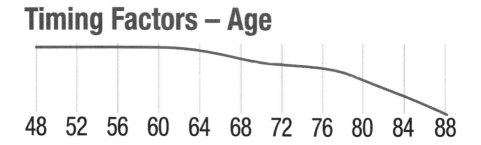

48 52 56 60 64 68 72 76 80 84 88

It has a lot to do with the fact that we may or may not have the energy, desire or vitality to continue to operate the business. Our focus may be on other personal or charitable pursuits.

The older one gets, the higher the chance of health problems, memory loss and other matters. This can impact your productivity.

From an effective transition perspective, if you are an older entrepreneur, more than likely you may not want to stick around to help the buyer transition and grow the business for an extended period. In many cases, the businesses of older owners rely very heavily on their owners. They have been operating their companies for a long time and have not been able to exit until now.

In these types of cases, mortality risk alone during an extended transition period can add sizeable risk for the buyer. Either he or she will walk away or want a substantially reduced price and highly favorable terms.

Business Stage

If you are a startup vs. a growth company vs. a mature business vs. a declining business, the stage of your business can have a material impact on your exit valuation. If you are a growth business, you will likely command a higher multiple vs. a business that is mature and/or declining.

Timing Factors – Business Stage

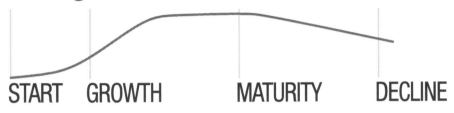

START   GROWTH   MATURITY   DECLINE

Deal Activity

What is happening in the market can impact value as well. If there is a robust merger and acquisition cycle and plenty of easily available capital, it will contribute to higher multiples.

Timing Factors – Deal Activity

1 2 3 4 5 6 7 8 9 10 11 12 13 14 15

The merger and acquisition cycle changes every few years and while it does not follow some guaranteed trend line, it seems to peak or dip every 5-7 years. During the dips, the money supply may get very tight. During the financial crisis of 2007-2008, it was hard to get financing and, no matter how great the company, the valuation multiples came down.

It is no different than a buying a house. When interest rates are low, buyers can afford to pay at the top end of the valuation range and still be able to manage their mortgage payments.

Business-for-Sale Inventory

This has not been a timing issue until now, but the coming Baby Boomer Business Sell-Off will dramatically impact value and flood the market with business-for-sale inventory. This is expected to turn the market into the mother of all buyer's markets. It is a phenomenon that has never been seen before and could have dramatic consequences. It is an understatement to describe it as the biggest business sell-off in American history.

Seasonality and Cyclicality

Does your company produce a significant chunk of its revenue during a certain time of the year? For example, a ski resort will do the bulk of its business during the winter months. This can drive down the multiple, especially if the buyer is acquiring after the season has just ended. That's seasonality.

Are your company's revenues overly impacted by the economic cycle? Certain cyclical and commodity companies are very dependent on commodity prices and/or the economy. Their valuation can get impacted due to economic and commodity pricing characteristics vs. their own company-specific characteristics. Examples of this would be oil companies and the price of oil, or housing and automobile sectors in a down economy. That's cyclicality.

Business Environment

The business environment can be a huge factor when trying to exit your business. I am referring to capital gains tax rates, interest rates, stock market fluctuations and downturns, currency fluctuations, corporate belt tightening, the P/E ratios of public companies using their P/E ratios as leverage – all of which can impact merger and acquisition activity.

Best Time to Exit?

Ideally, the best time to exit a business is when you are so sure of your company's prospects that you wouldn't dream of selling. When you are the most bullish about your company's prospects, it is generally the time you can get maximum value.

However, many entrepreneurs wait until it's too late to exit. The phenomenon is not much different than holding investments for too long in the stock market. We don't cash in our chips because we have our eye on the potential value of tomorrow. Ever been ahead at the tables in Vegas only to lose it all and then some?

Be careful not to get bogged down with your operator-specific issues. I recently ran across an entrepreneur who had some payroll tax issues with the IRS and his entire reason for not wanting to exit had to do with the fact that he owed payroll taxes.

Remember, your obligations are operator specific (that means YOU) and may not necessarily have anything to do with the business fundamentals. In the case of the entrepreneur I mentioned, the payroll taxes were from an issue several years prior. The buyer simply paid off the IRS as part of purchase price consideration.

As with many other things in life, your timing in selling your company will be key if you want to get the best sale price. Keep a careful eye on the market. Industry changes, such as consolidations, rollups, regulatory hurdles, taxes etc., can impact your company value positively or negatively.

To maximize value at exit time, I recommend that your business have three years of financials that are on a positive trend line. By that I mean, growing revenues and profits.

The bottom line is simply this: You cannot time everything perfectly.

If you don't have three years of positive financial trend line, don't lose heart. Do the best you can. Set a value. Assess that value. Look at milestones along the way. Watch out for the valuation multiples in your industry. Stay objective. Be ready when the time comes.

Chapter 29.

Net Proceeds: "The Real Wake-Up Call" for Entrepreneurs

Net proceeds is essentially the number you will walk away with after satisfying all obligations, liabilities and taxes from your business sale.

There is one thing you need to know:

No matter what net proceeds number you calculate prior to sale, there is a decent likelihood that you will collect a much lower amount.

This is because all kinds of transaction variables and price adjustments have yet to play out.

Entrepreneurs are generally unaware of the complex world of the M&A transaction, so they tend to over-simplify the net proceeds calculation and wake up to a nasty surprise mid-transaction or a harsh reality post-closing.

That's because most entrepreneurs rarely think in terms of what is the consideration; what are the other components making up the purchase price offered by the buyer beyond the cash. For example, a portion of the purchase price could be in seller notes, earn-out or some other type of deferred or contingent payments.

Let's keep going.

Beyond consideration, there is risk allocation.

Often, 5-25% of sale proceeds can sit in escrow for 6-24 months depending on the buyer's perceived risk in the transaction. This further reduces your net proceeds number for a period of time.

Depending on how long the escrow period is and how much cash was paid upfront and when taxes are due, this can create quite the liquidity pinch for you.

This liquidity pinch can get worse if surprise tax implications pop up in the form of depreciation recapture, which is subject to ordinary income tax rates or higher tax implications of non-compete payments. (Remember: Not all sale proceeds are taxed at capital gains rates.)

Most entrepreneurs don't realize the tremendous costs associated with preparing and divesting the company. These can include value enhancement initiatives, clean up and preparation costs, advisory fees, transaction marketing fees, due diligence fees, legal fees, accounting fees, commissions and winding-down costs associated with excluded items.

Many of these can further drive down the net proceeds – and this is before the purchase price adjustments even come into play.

Before or after closing, there may be purchase price adjustments for working capital, taxes, off balance sheet liabilities, non-accrued liabilities, product warranty claims etc. In most cases, these will reduce the purchase price and may subsequently reduce the escrow account dollar for dollar.

Basically, a portion of the money you were counting on simply does not materialize. In some cases, you may have to give back some of the money that has already been given to you.

By the time the entrepreneur really gets a net, net, net number, there can be sizeable shortfall and it can be a tremendous shocker, especially because some of this may happen after a binding agreement is signed.

Think you are done? Nope.

Then comes the big surprise. These are all the exclusions (liabilities and obligations that the buyer did not assume) that may have slipped below the radar and can really add up.

Entrepreneurs don't think in terms of exclusions. By exclusions, I mean those liabilities you will still be stuck with after the sale. These exclusions can have a sizeable impact on the net proceeds amount that you collect.

Most entrepreneurs tend to think of their business as an entity that will be sold lock, stock and barrel. The buyer, on the other hand, wants to cherry pick key assets and related operating liabilities that truly benefit the go forward enterprise.

The entrepreneur can be left with a whole bag of liabilities that he or she never thought about.

Exclusions

Unpaid Taxes	Excluded Liabilities Through Date of Closing	Environmental Liabilities
Liabilities Related to an Excluded Asset	Trade Payables Through Date of Closing	Employment Claims Through Date of Closing
Seller Guaranteed Debts	Excluded Debts	Excluded Leases

Before the sale, I generally go through the client's financials, review assets and liabilities, and prepare a list of everything that is likely not to be assumed by buyer. In some cases, the amount can be so large that the entrepreneur may not want to sell because he or she needs the business cash flow to sustain the debt service on those liabilities.

Not all liabilities are the same. Remember that operating liabilities benefit the buyer. Non-operating liabilities benefit the seller and generally don't aid operations and will likely not be assumed by the buyer.

So be careful and understand the full implications – especially when you're trying to negotiate off personal guarantees and a portion of those guarantees encompasses non-operating liabilities that the buyer may not assume.

Make your own list of all your company's liabilities. Be clear that if you were to sell your business, what liabilities will be assumed.

Chapter 30.

Preparing Mentally to Give Up Control

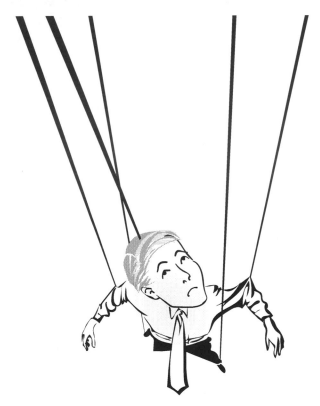

Giving up control of a business – particularly a business that one has built – can be very devastating emotionally for the entrepreneur. Often he or she has paid little mind to giving up control and is not ready for the consequences.

Entrepreneurs really like to be in control. So it's not surprising that they have issues after the sale and have difficulty adjusting to their new reality regardless of how big the check they received.

Often, after selling the business, the entrepreneur ends up being an employee along with other employees who were formerly his or her subordinates. It's a difficult adjustment.

In a situation like that, many entrepreneurs can't wait to leave. The problem magnifies because they don't stick around to harvest the earn-out period or have difficulties satisfying their post-closing obligations. Sometimes that gets them in a whole lot of financial trouble. Often they leave money on the table.

Our view when selling is, usually, "Cut me a big enough check and, sure, I will play your game for a while." The problem is that we can be unrealistic about our capacity to deal with bureaucratic crap and buyer demands. This can cost big money.

Beyond becoming an employee of the company you once owned, loss of control manifests in many other ways. For example, there's immense emotional toll and frustration seeing terminations and reshuffling of people who were your loyal employees.

It doesn't stop at employees. It goes to important customers, too. Customers that you valued – the ones who helped you build your business, supported you over the years and stuck with you. All of a sudden, they are calling you because their prices are going up and you have no control over the situation and limited to no ability to help them.

It could also be suppliers who stood by you for decades. All of a sudden they are being let go or being asked to dramatically reduce prices, and they're calling you for help.

Many times this loss of control hits on an entirely different level and taints the entrepreneur's business legacy. In other cases, companies that have existed in the family for generations get acquired and are absorbed in a larger enterprise and the company name is no longer there.

In some cases, the shocks can be felt even if you leave the company.

You'd be surprised by how many entrepreneurs I've talked to who cannot believe that they signed the non-compete agreement that they did. An overwhelming majority tell me that they cannot wait for their non-compete to expire. They literally count down the days.

My message is this: Do some soul searching and recognize the realities. Understand that you are being given a big check and that the new company has an entirely different agenda than yours.

Too often, entrepreneurs get overly optimistic about the future of the company they sold and have high expectations from the buyer. This is a trap and, most likely, you will be let down.

If you park your expectations at the door and focus on making yourself part of the solution instead a part of the problem, you'll be just fine. Fighting it and being a rebel is not advisable. Expect bureaucracy, tedious tasks and micro-management (among other things) if you agree to stay on with the company. If you expect it, you will adjust better.

Also expect change: A lot of change. Your company will likely get a change-over from the top down.

Look at this way. Someone just bought your house. The house you grew up in. If they want to remodel it, paint it or demolish it, it is their asset and their right. Get over it and get yourself into an asset-oriented mindset. That'll help you let go.

Chapter 31.

Exit Expertise

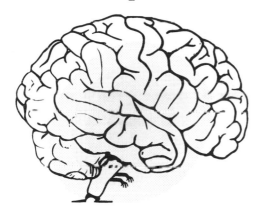

Stop me if you've heard this before but most entrepreneurs sell a business once in a lifetime whereas buyers are in the market on a regular basis.

This means that there's an expertise gap between seller and buyer. And many buyers are prepared to take advantage of it. Especially with sellers who think they have expertise but really don't.

Most entrepreneur sellers have expertise gaps at two levels.

The Exit Options Expertise Gap

Entrepreneurs are often unaware of what their exit options are and which exit channel best suits their personal, family, financial and business objectives. It's very important to undergo an exercise to identify your exit options.

Exit options can be grouped into internal or external exit options. Here are both:

Internal Exit Options

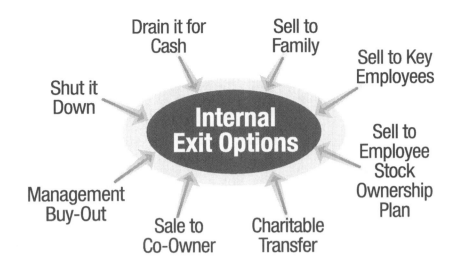

External Exit Options

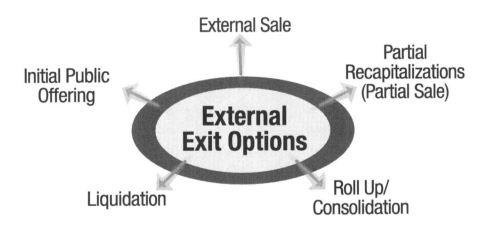

Unfortunately, most entrepreneurs lack the expertise to do a realistic exit-options analysis to understand what their exit options are. Many don't understand the connection between the exit channel and their valuation.

As I mentioned earlier in the book, every exit channel, whether you are selling to employees or selling to third-party buyers, likely has a different valuation (essentially a different price), different potential tax implications and a different set of liabilities and exposures that are unique to that exit channel.

What I see as the prevalent problem is that the entrepreneur has most likely never used the words "exit" and "channel" together. Neither does he or she know their relevance to their financial ambitions.

Most of us simply want to sell our businesses. Who knew there were multiple valuations for the same business depending on the exit channel? Or that there were such things as "multiple valuations" and "exit channels"?

The Merger and Acquisition Expertise Gap

You, the entrepreneur, are an expert on your business. You know it better than anyone else. You know your products. (Why wouldn't you? You most likely created them.) You are the one operating the business. You are as close to being an expert on your business as it comes.

But operating a business and divesting it are two different matters.

Buyers know how to sock it to the selling entrepreneur – and don't think they won't. It's a dog eat dog world, my friend. Be advised.

The problem gets worse when negotiating with multiple buyers, complicated terms and understanding of the real impact of the proposed transactions structures.

This is where an experienced advisor will be indispensable to you in designing a transaction that will be acceptable to both you and the buyer. Besides, the right advisor will be both your guide through the selling process and your valuable intermediary when dealing with multiple buyers.

There are all kinds of advisors that can help you mitigate your risk and improve the outcome. Here are a few:

One of the problems is that we entrepreneurs are fee adverse. We don't want to pay for something if we think we can handle it ourselves.

If I tell you to create a team of advisors, you'll probably roll your eyes. That would be a mistake.

There are times you pay fees and times you don't. This is one of the times you pay. Bite the bullet and get all of your advisors together and make sure everyone is on the same page.

I am not saying don't keep a close eye on fees. What I am saying is that assembling and listening to the right kinds of advisors will likely make a huge difference in having more money in your pocket, paying less in taxes, keeping your money protected and aligning your personal, family and financial goals with your business goals.

The Transaction

Chapter 32.

Selling the Buyer

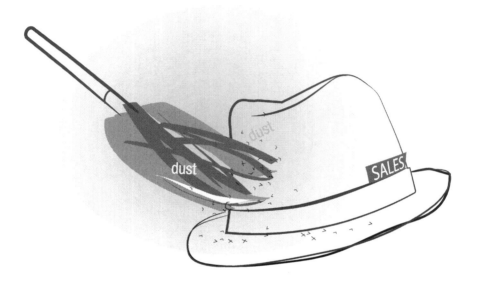

Building a Business Case

Remember when you first started your business and you needed capital? And you were out hustling for money? When you had that sales hat on and wouldn't take "no" for an answer?

The people you were pitching to were investors and you had to be ready. You had business plans, operational plans, financial models . . . everything it would take to raise capital.

What most entrepreneurs don't realize is that the people who buy companies are investors. Just like the people you may have pitched for capital to start your company.

Somehow most entrepreneurs don't seem to view buyers that way. If they did, they would prepare differently. Your buyer is an investor who is looking for a rate of return. And the average entrepreneur is very complacent with these buyers.

What the entrepreneur should be doing is selling the buyer on the future potential of their company.

Buyers will often demand a business and growth plan. How else are they supposed to vet the feasibility of your growth strategy? Having documented plans allows you to build your business case with the buyer; clearly demonstrating how the company will grow topline revenues, sustain margins and profits. This will help improve or sustain exit valuation.

For the record, I hate business plans with colorful charts in big binders that sit on shelves collecting dust. Keep your plan real. Keep it short and keep it actionable.

Think of your plans as maps for the buyers. Without these, it is difficult for the buyer to understand the full scope of the value of your opportunity. Remember: We don't sell our businesses, we sell our opportunity. Therefore, preparing a sizzling business case to convince the buyer of the potential of your business and the underlying opportunity is paramount to maximizing exit value.

Aligning the Story

Make sure that you are developing a good story for the buyer. Imagine that one day the buyer comes in and starts interviewing your employees. The ideal narrative that your employees should be delivering is that, "He rarely comes in, and when he does it's for manager meetings.

He seems to play a lot of golf." That is a good story and it shows the buyer that the business has legs outside of the entrepreneur.

To get in the habit, I often tell my clients to get out of the office and work from somewhere else. I recommend they stop coming into the office unless being there is strategically important or mission critical for the survival for the business.

The buyer will ask many different types of questions as to why you're exiting your business. Many entrepreneurs are simply not prepared for these questions.

Not only do I want you to be prepared to answer the questions decisively, I want your employees and key management people to be able to deliver something equally decisive.

What you don't want is that when the buyer asks why you're exiting, you say something like, "My wife wants us to travel more." And your key manager says, "I think our industry is on a real downtrend and who knows whether we will have our biggest customers next year." That right there is the kiss of death: Two of them, in fact.

Creating Competition

For lower middle market to middle-market companies and up, the selling price is almost never named. The market decides the price. In smaller companies, however, you will find business listings with a sale price – especially if the company is working with a business broker.

Once your company gets to be a certain size, the price is almost never revealed. Your M&A advisors will typically run an informal merger and acquisition process or a private auction to engage various buyers to drive up purchase price.

Many entrepreneurs confuse the private auction process with a public auction. This is not the same thing. This is a private process with a group of buyers that are highly targeted. In a formal private auction, access is provided to key financial materials through virtual data rooms etc., and buyers must submit bids by a certain date – whereas in the informal M&A process, competitive tension is created to play potential buyers against each other to improve the offering price.

However, if you, the entrepreneur, find that this type process makes you uncomfortable, just remember that you are in control. You can always say no to the offer. But why limit yourself?

Not limiting your options is especially important when a synergistic buyer could swoop in at the right time and potentially pay you a lot more than what you initially thought for the company.

Many buyers balk at this kind of competitive process, especially strategic buyers who are generally corporate acquirers, as well as many financial buyers. For these groups, attempting to create competition is commonly a no-win situation.

If the buyer participates in the auction, either the buyer ends up paying too much or ends up being the losing bidder; walking away after having spent time and resources with nothing to show for it.

When dealing with multiple buyers, an advisor's role should be to not only to drive up the purchase price, but also to negotiate and improve the terms. Here are a few things a good advisor will have on his or her radar:

The Role of a Competent Advisor

Increase Upfront Cash Amount	Minimize Earn-Outs	Reduce/ Eliminate Seller Financing
Optimize Transaction Structure	Optimize Tax Impact	Improve Key Terms & Conditions
Optimize Post Transaction Involvement	Lower Escrow/ Holdback Amounts	Speed Up Closing Times

Remember, your motivation for selling is almost always different from the reason the buyer wants to purchase your company.

In many cases, buyers have hidden agendas that, when enacted, can have huge revenue potential for the buyer. With competition, they are forced to pay a pretty penny to ensure that they don't lose out on the deal they really want.

Chapter 33.

Dealing With the Human Obstacles

When buyers and entrepreneurs – sometimes with the assistance of their advisors – all start butting heads and protecting their respective turfs, the ruckus can create all kinds of disputes and lead to tremendous transaction stress.

Often, it is simply a case of missing competencies in the buyer, the entrepreneur and/or deficiencies within their advisors because of their lack of experience.

Sometimes, attorneys can be very passionate in their quest to protect their client. Keep your attorneys aligned with your end goal. An attorney playing an, "I gotta have my way at all costs" game can be very costly for you. Lawyers on both sides tend to get bogged down in issues that can blow up the deal.

Keep in mind that long after the attorney is gone, you still have to work with the buyer. If this is happening, talk to your attorney and get the situation resolved.

In the M&A world, the deal falls apart a few times before it gets done and a smart advisor will filter information and protect the entrepreneur from the constant bombardment of comments made between the buy side and the sell side. Also, many times advisors do not keep control and have little visibility over the transaction process. As a result, important elements get sidelined, there's missing information, unnecessary delays, hurt feelings, outright rage and anger, especially when there are a lot of egos involved.

For us entrepreneurs, some of our biggest strengths start getting in our way. We like to talk and in many cases, we end up talking too much. Even though we may hire competent advisors, we're used to being in control and we like to second-guess our advisors and, in some cases, even go behind their backs.

If we ever meet in person, ask me about the story of the entrepreneur who cost himself $475,000 by second-guessing his advisor.

We're impatient. So we don't have a lot of patience with the sale process, which could stretch on for six to twelve months or more. Often we can be egotistical and there are ego clashes between us and the buyer. This does nobody any good.

The successful sale of your business is not a contest. Try and be as patient as possible – negotiations are more like a game of chess than running a 100-yard dash.

Remember: You may be right, but you may also end up not selling your company.

Chapter 34.
Letter of Intent

Entrepreneurs are very focused on getting the maximum price possible for their business. Why shouldn't we be? We're entrepreneurs. We're opportunistic. We make lemonade out of sour lemons. Right?

The problem is that when you're selling your business the purchase price has a huge stick of C4 attached to it. If you focus only on the price and not on the attached C4 explosive, you're going to have a substantial problem on your hands. More than likely a good portion of your wealth will get blown up.

What am I talking about?

When selling a business, the purchase price comes with strings attached. These strings are "total consideration being offered" and "terms and conditions." In many cases, it may be better to take a lower purchase price with better terms than a higher purchase price with really onerous terms.

Consideration is the total amount of money that is offered for the transaction. However, there are a lot of gotcha factors and complexities in consideration.

Beyond cash, consideration could be of all kinds. As part of the consideration, the buyer could assume certain debts directly or repay certain debts on your behalf. The buyer could offer a portion of his or her company stock as a consideration as well. Often you hear about public companies acquiring other companies for cash payments plus their publicly traded stock. This is an example of consideration as well.

Many times the consideration can be contingent on certain elements. A common example of contingent consideration is earn-outs. Earn-outs are often used to bridge the valuation gap between buyers and sellers. Contingent consideration can also be based upon the renewal of a key customer contract or key licensing agreement that is mission critical for the future success of your company.

There's an old adage that says "seller's price and buyer's terms." The buyers will propose the purchase price and the underlying terms in a letter of intent. The wisest thing the entrepreneur can do is to NOT think of the purchase price as a standalone item. Instead of negotiating purchase price, the entrepreneur should negotiate the letter of intent. The letter of intent generally includes the price, key terms, proposed structure, allocation of risk i.e. earn-outs, escrows etc.

A key thing to remember with a letter of intent is that the moment you accept and sign on that dotted line, the only thing that can likely happen to the purchase price is that it can go down.

This is because you lose your leverage with the buyer the second you sign a letter of intent. So it's important that you do the heavy lifting prior to accepting the letter of intent.

By signing the letter of intent there are two things that have happened. First, you have permitted due diligence to commence. Second, the buyer most likely will use this juncture to start talking to third-party lenders to finance the transaction. It is imperative that if you've got issues within your business that you haven't disclosed, that you disclose these items to the buyer long before you sign the letter of intent.

When preparing your business for sale prior to listing it, you should make a list of all things that need to be fixed. My rule is identify and rectify. The items that cannot be rectified you should keep on a list. The items on that list need to be disclosed to the buyer before any letter of intent is signed. That's because the last thing we want to do is to be several months into due diligence and something we knew about blows up the transaction. We've wasted time, effort, money and hassle for nothing.

Buyers are very smart. Their advisors are generally very competent and they will go through your company's records and look at every nook and cranny. If you haven't disclosed everything – including something you'd rather not disclose – more than likely it will come out.

Get a good attorney to draft and/or review the letter of intent. A letter of intent is typically a non-binding document with a couple of exceptions. Generally, the only binding elements of a letter of intent are "exclusivity," which means that you will not shop your deal in the market for a certain number of months and "confidentiality," which means that all information will be keep confidential. That said, be careful with unintended binding elements. Even though the letter of intent is a non-binding document, you still have a responsibility to act in good faith.

My message is don't be swayed by price alone. When it comes to selling your business, the best thing you can do is get out of the mindset of negotiating purchase price and get into the mindset of negotiating a letter of intent. An isolated view of the purchase price by itself is a disaster waiting to happen.

While it is mission critical to negotiate the key aspects of the deal at the letter of intent stage, keep in mind, just because a buyer wants to enter into a letter of intent to purchase your company, that doesn't mean the deal will get done. With the signing of a letter of intent, all you are really doing is agreeing to negotiate a definitive purchase and sale agreement in good faith. This purchase and sale agreement will govern the terms and conditions of the sale transaction and until this is negotiated and subsequently signed, there is no deal.

Chapter 35.
Risk Allocation

Smart entrepreneurs focus on building a great business. The really wise ones work on making sure that the business is not only great but can also operate without the entrepreneur. But one thing most never realize is that when it comes to selling the business, almost everything becomes largely about risk allocation.

What do I mean?

Most entrepreneurs I meet want to walk off into the sunset with 100% of their money upfront without any obligation to the buyer beyond some short period of time to transition the business. That is the ideal exit scenario, especially if you are burnt out or ready to move toward the next chapter of your life.

On the other hand, the buyer wants to pay the entrepreneur as little cash as possible with the entrepreneur financing as much of the transaction as possible. The buyer also wants the entrepreneur on the hook for everything and tries to build in every possible recourse (ideally, with no liability caps) if the entrepreneur has misrepresented or underrepresented material things.

Simply put, the buyer is concerned about all kinds of deal unknowns that could lower the buyer's rate of return and negatively impact their purchase dramatically.

Now I am going to say something that may surprise you.

All Cash = Lower Price

What I mean is that if you want to get 100% of your cash up front, you will likely get offered the lowest purchase price possible.

Price generally depends on the consideration offered, and the terms and conditions and the transaction structure proposed. If the buyer is offering contingent consideration or deferred consideration in the form of an earn-out or deferred payments, the purchase price will most likely be higher.

If the buyer is shifting risk to the seller by proposing very broad language in representations and warranties backed up with a significant escrow, the price will most likely be higher. If the buyer perceives tax advantages, that also will help improve the purchase price.

Beyond wanting 100% of their cash upfront, many entrepreneurs seem to fixate on an "AS IS" price. I often run across entrepreneurs that will make statements along the lines of, "Well, my company is what it is and that's how

I want to sell it." It's kind of a "You can kick the tires but I'm not budging on my price" attitude.

I'm here to tell you that an "as is" price may not benefit you. It may actually lower your price.

"AS IS" Sale = Lower Price

In many situations, it makes little to no sense to ask for an "as is" price. You will be taking less money unnecessarily. If you agree to a purchase price and you don't hold to this "as is" standard, your purchase price would likely be higher because the buyer can shift risk to you.

Remember, if there is a significant problem that comes up before the transaction is closed, the buyer can ask for a price revision anyway. In fact, the buyer has traditional safeguards in the Purchase and Sale Agreement. He or she can lower the purchase price even after the transaction has closed by making purchase price adjustments per the Purchase and Sale Agreement.

Why automatically go for an "as is" price? In my mind, you're needlessly getting less money when there's a reasonable chance that you can get more money doing it the other way.

In some cases, a seller can pull off an "as is" price without impact to the purchase price. It really depends on the buyer motivation. If the buyer wants your company badly enough, or if you find yourself in a robust seller's market, you can use that to your advantage beyond an "as is" price by negotiating less restrictive representations, warranties and covenants and also heavily negotiate the form of consideration and other terms.

If you look under the hood of a normal sale transaction, you will find that the transaction structure, consideration and terms and conditions are a function of risk allocation. Earn-outs, seller notes, escrows, clawbacks, purchase price adjustments and others are common methods of risk allocation. If your advisors have not negotiated proper indemnification caps, the buyer could potentially transfer unlimited liability to you.

Many times, the buyer will insist on having merger and acquisition insurance for certain breaches of representations and warranties. Other examples of risk allocation are excluding product warranty claims and employment claims through date of closing as well as many other types of liabilities from the purchase price – thus leaving the entrepreneur holding the bag.

All of these are negotiating points that many entrepreneurs never see coming because they have no education in them and are simply not prepared to deal with them effectively. Not only do they not know what they are looking for, in some cases, they may not have the right advisor and may end up with a lot of unintended consequences.

Chapter 36.

Transaction Structure and Taxes

Why Buyers Buy Assets Rather than Stock

The bulk of M&A transactions in the United States are structured as asset purchases, so there's a high likelihood that the buyer is going to want to buy some, most or all of your company's assets rather than the stock of your company.

In a stock type purchase, the buyer generally does not get the significant tax benefits that he would get in an asset purchase.

The buyer gains various advantages by structuring the transaction as an asset purchase such as:

1. The buyer can pick and choose the specific assets she wants to buy.

2. The buyer can pick and choose the liabilities she wants to assume and disregard the rest.

3. The buyer can reduce the tax bite by allocating the purchase price to specific asset classes and taking advantage of depreciation and amortization timetables.

4. The buyer's net outlay for the purchase price may be less due to tax advantages.

5. In some cases for the buyer, it's easier to get financing because the financing may be tied to certain specific assets.

6. The buyer can buy certain assets and move them into a new structure without being stuck with the previous company's trailing liabilities and legacy issues.

Taxes can become the Achilles heel in transactions. Put yourself in the shoes of the buyer. The buyer is an investor looking for a return on investment and, in many cases, has used third-party financing to fund the purchase of your business.

Without tax benefits, the buyer can be dramatically impacted, especially in the early stage of the transaction, when, if he or she doesn't get the tax benefits, it decreases cash flow and lowers the rate of return.

Buyers are very smart and they want their own tax advantages. In the absence of these, they will likely walk away or offer a reduced purchase price. Therefore, it is imperative for the entrepreneur to sit down with his or her tax advisor to optimize the company's tax position and ensure a tax-neutral corporate structure many years prior to an exit.

Many entrepreneurs end up paying a lot more tax than they need to because they don't optimize their tax position. You've already heard me preach about the entrepreneur doing tax planning at the closing table. If you've been paying attention, you know that by then it's too late.

My point is that the buyer's taxes also matter. Many entrepreneurs make the mistake of only thinking about their own taxes. A tax neutral structure allows for more flexibility when working with buyers who are less likely to walk away if they can maximize their own tax advantages.

Most entrepreneurs have a disconnect with how important structure is to the valuation. As I mentioned earlier, in the case of C-corporations this is a real problem because this structure would subject them to multiple levels of taxation, which would include tax at the corporate level, individual level and the state level depending on the state of residence.

So, why the prevalence of C-corporations for small business? While there are legitimate reasons for having one, for many it is because that's how they started initially and nothing has happened to get them to change.

The only time I really see stock transactions coming into play in an M&A transaction is when a buyer wants to acquire your company and there is a really strong reason for him to buy your stock instead of your assets because it benefits him in some material way.

It could be that your intellectual property is so compelling and so important to the buyer that he is willing to forgo the tax benefits and be stuck with potential unknown liabilities of the business.

More often than not, I see a C-corporation stock being purchased when a company has hard to get licenses or contracts, which cannot be transferred and are specific to the corporation.

The problem does not vanish if you want to change your C-corporation to an S-corporation. There's a 10-year built-in-gains-taxes time clock that starts when you do. That is, if you were to sell your business in that ten-year period, you would still be subject to a double tax on the built-in-gain portion of the sales proceeds.

What's more, buyers tend to take advantage of purchase price allocations, often to the entrepreneur's detriment. Buyers are going to take the purchase price and allocate it against various asset classes/categories of your business. They will allocate the most they can to any asset class or category with the most tax benefit to them.

For example, they would likely want to allocate what they could to equipment that has an up to 7-year depreciation cycle vs. goodwill, which has a 15-year amortization cycle.

While this may feel like an exercise in semantics to the entrepreneur, it could have real serious repercussions and can cost him or her dearly in the form of a higher tax bill. For example, when the buyer allocates part of the purchase price to equipment, it could be that the entrepreneur's company has previously depreciated its equipment above its cost basis and is subject to depreciation recapture, which is taxed at the ordinary (maximum) tax rate.

Also, it is entirely possible that a fair portion of the sales proceeds were allocated to non-compete payments. Non-compete payments can have a higher potential tax impact for the entrepreneur.

The deal structure and resulting taxes can make or break a transaction. Depending on the transaction structure and your entity type, you could have substantial tax problems on your hands.

I have talked to entrepreneurs who have found out about adverse tax consequences after they have signed a binding purchase and sale agreement. By that time, it's too late in the process to back out.

Remember: It's not the buyer's job to advise you of your tax consequences. Buyers will almost always structure the purchase of your company for their benefit, which may be to your detriment.

The time to optimize your tax position is many years prior to sale. A simple planning session with your tax advisors may one day save you a boatload of heartache at the closing table.

Chapter 37.
Earn-Outs

Let's say that you and the buyer are negotiating price. You are very, very bullish about your company. You believe your company is worth a lot more than the buyer is offering. It could be either because of legitimate reasons – perhaps you have a new product that you're launching and you think that your sales could triple in the next couple of years – or it could be that you have entirely unrealistic expectations around your business value and its future.

The buyer wants to get the deal closed but he needs to bridge the valuation gap between you and them. That's when the earn-out rears its head.

The earn-out means that all associated future payments are contingent on the performance of the business calculated using an agreed upon formula between you and the buyer.

The problem is that many earn-outs do not materialize.

A lot of it has to do with the fact that the entrepreneurs are novices when it comes to selling a business and, in many cases, the advisors may not push hard enough.

You will hear some advisors say things like "Let's get as much money upfront as we can. The earn-out . . . who knows? There are too many ways to get screwed. So if it happens, consider the earn-out gravy."

While I don't disagree with the above, I also believe it is hard to negotiate an effective earn-out with that mindset.

I have had many cases where my clients have collected substantial earn-outs. In one case alone, an effectively structured earn-out yielded over $30 million.

That said, more often than not, earn-outs don't materialize.

When you are banking on the future performance of the company, it's one thing when you are in control. It's an entirely different thing when someone else is in control.

If your earn-out is based on net earnings of the business, then you might as well forget about it because it's too easy to change the expense mix of the company. The new owner might add a bunch of expenses for all kinds of things to lower the earnings of the company.

When I'm negotiating an earn-out for a client, I want to stay as close to the top revenue line as possible. Ideally, I want a percentage of the top line revenue. If I cannot get the buyer to agree to a percent of the top line revenue, then I want to be at the gross margin or gross profit line.

But once you go below that, you are dealing with all kinds of operating expenses and it is a murky world. It's hard to keep from getting screwed in all that muck.

That said, if the buyer is insistent upon paying the earn-out based on profits, it is imperative that you agree to a budget with the buyer and isolate all expenses and reasonable percentage variances of those expenses, so that if the buyer tries to change the make-up of the expenses or tries to increase expenses, advertently or inadvertently, you are reasonably insulated.

It is also critical that the entrepreneur have control over elements that ensure performance. Let's say your company just sold. The first thing that's going to happen is that a bunch of your employees will be reshuffled or let go because the buyer is going to harvest cost synergies. Automatically, your culture will change and everyone in the organization will be dealing with red tape and bureaucracy.

Buyers are generally very synergy focused. To realize cost synergies, they will consolidate all kinds of functions into their existing company operations. An example of this is that your marketing team gets reshuffled into the buyer's main company and the sales team remains in your business unit. Now your sales team gets supported by the marketing team whose mandate may or may not be aligned with the sales team's. That usually leads to bad communication, lackluster results and frustration.

Meanwhile, you are tearing your hair out and nothing is getting done. You are helpless – especially when you're the one who stands to lose a nice chunk of the sale proceeds you were counting on.

Be sure to deal with the issue of debt. Often in the case of financial buyers, the company can get quickly saddled with a lot of debt. It is quite normal for your perfectly healthy company to get substantially leveraged because of the buyer's capital structure.

It's entirely possible that there's no money to pay you even if you have delivered on your earn-out. This could be because of massive new debt interest payments and other reasons.

Make certain that you have some stipulations on the revenue side as well. I am referring to a "what constitutes revenue" clause.

I had lunch with an entrepreneur recently who told me yet another horror story about his earn-out, which was based on hitting revenue milestones. The entrepreneur's company was acquired by its largest customer. The buyer was a public company and, after the acquisition, consolidated manufacturing into the parent company to get better cost synergies.

The entrepreneur's company had been getting $250/ unit from the customer prior to the sale, but the buyer's changes dropped the price to $93/unit. This caused over 50% reduction in revenue for the entrepreneur's former company.

Guess what that did to the entrepreneur's earn-out?

Chapter 38.

Due Diligence: How and Why the Buyer Uses it to Lower Sale Price

I guarantee that if you ever saw a due diligence checklist or a due diligence request by a decent acquirer, you would panic. The first time I saw one, albeit it was ages ago, I nearly had a fit.

The bulk of entrepreneurs I have met underestimate due diligence and its impact on their business, their employees and themselves.

They are not prepared for the level of scrutiny, the extended time frame or the time commitment required of the entrepreneur and certain key players. Neither are they ready for the associated costs – both in hard costs and in terms of distractions and disruptions that could potentially impact the company's momentum.

Many entrepreneurs choose to be very reactive about due diligence. That can create a lot of problems for them. For starters, it can blindside the business with all kinds of problems that management is not prepared for. Typically, the entrepreneur is busy putting out fires and isn't aware that the company is laden with all kinds of issues, deficiencies, liabilities and risks.

That said, due diligence is not just about finding your company's deficiencies, risks and liabilities. The process is a mission critical part of helping the buyer validate and revalidate his acquisition motivation and strategy relative to the opportunity that your company presents. The following diagram shows the buyer's due diligence mindset:

In the process of due diligence the buyer will request a mountain of data. When I say a mountain of data, I mean it. Due diligence generally involves four functional risk categories:

1. **Financial Statement Risk**

2. **Legal and Compliance Risk**

3. **Operational and Management Risk**

4. **Transactional Risk (which covers documents and the transaction itself)**

The next diagram shows these categories broken down into various sub-categories. If this does not get your attention, please note that there are often dozens of line items of data requests under each one of these sub-categories.

Examples: Due Diligence Categories

Corporate Information	Capitalization	Financial & Tax
Operations & Capacity	Payroll & Benefits	Employees & Management
Customers Suppliers	Balance Sheet Information	Insurance
Debts & Obligations	Real Property	Business Personal Property
Regulatory	Product Claims Warranty/ Liability	Lawsuits & Disputes
Industry Specific	Environmental	Governmental
Information Technology		Intellectual Property/ R&D

The buyer will go through due diligence with a fine-tooth comb. He or she has two purposes for doing this:

1. To ensure that she is not getting screwed and is getting what she's paying for.

2. The buyer is using your data to assess the opportunity as well as looking for opportunities to lower his purchase price. Buy-side advisors representing their clients do their utmost to earn their keep by helping uncover opportunities to reduce the purchase price.

Prior to sale, I advise you to hire a competent attorney to conduct the process of legal due diligence which looks at everything from UCC1 filings (liens) to key legal agreements and leases. You really don't want surprises that are out of your control at the closing table.

Due diligence can be very costly and cause a lot of distractions and disruptions in the workplace. Deals often fall apart in due diligence because the entrepreneur has taken his or her foot off the gas and is so distracted with due diligence that it causes a loss of momentum in the business.

It is essential for you to hire a quarterback to manage the due diligence process. His or her job is to maintain and control the M&A process, working both with the sell-side and buy-side advisors and stakeholders.

A key point that some entrepreneurs often don't understand is their role in lender-driven due diligence. Often the mandate and the thrust of the due diligence extends beyond the buyer to the buyer's third-party lender who may be controlling the due diligence process by loan underwriting mandates.

It is essential for you to understand that as a part of

selling your business, you may play a role in facilitating lender-driven due diligence by making yourself available for lender presentations, interviews and clarifications while they're trying to underwrite the financing transaction.

Also, entrepreneurs often don't realize the role that their key employees could play in facilitating and supporting lender-driven due diligence. In most cases, the key employees would need to be a part of the team to get any transaction done.

Instead of resenting the due diligence process, look at due diligence in a more practical light. Imagine you're buying a house and you want to ensure the house does not have foundation problems, termite issues or other major issues that could set you back an arm and a leg. You get an inspection report done because you want to ensure that you are getting what you are paying for and that you're not taking any unnecessary risk.

In the process of due diligence, the buyer is trying to do exactly the same thing in making sure that when he buys the business it won't create any unnecessary risk for them or their shareholders.

Another thing the buyer is trying to ensure is that, after the transaction, he is not going to have major problems that are going to be cost prohibitive to deal with.

It is best to disclose any material fact or any material issue that could potentially occur. It is better to deal with risk disclosure (and potentially a purchase price reduction) than to deal with post-sale adjustments, clawbacks and litigation for undisclosed liabilities, under-reserved liabilities and misrepresentations. Risk disclosure before due diligence even begins is inexpensive. A lawsuit later won't be, and it will take away your peace of mind.

To speed up due diligence, make sure that there is a very clear timetable for requests. Keep a close tab on all information requests, timelines, completion dates and all exceptions and exception-related follow-ups.

Remember, due diligence should be a two-sided exercise. Before you sign a letter of intent with a potential buyer, you should ascertain where they get their capital and their financial worth. You should ask for references if he or she has previously bought companies and discuss the experience with other sellers.

You should do some work in understanding the buyer's company culture, what the buyer intends to do with your company and how all that will impact your employees and business momentum if the deal involves an earn-out.

If you will retain some ownership or have an earn-out, it is very important to discuss and understand how and who makes certain decisions and what the buyer's strategy is: Whether he will operate your business unit as a standalone unit, absorb it within the enterprise or create some other kind of hybrid model. Will the buyer be putting in operating capital? What is his access to additional capital?

A common reason cited for why acquisitions fail is because the buyer cut corners in performing due diligence by not putting enough importance on the process. For buyers, due diligence is a safety net. It is an excellent way to minimize surprises.

Rest assured that the buyer will likely take due diligence very seriously. Preparing for due diligence effectively requires cleanup and optimization. The process should begin many months, if not a year or more, in advance of an exit. Anything less can result in exit value destruction.

So, what happens if the buyer finds something adverse in the due diligence process and you haven't disclosed it?

Or maybe you didn't know about it. Maybe there's a revenue recognition issue. Maybe your bookkeeper made a significant error and it made your earnings higher than they actually were. Maybe there are bigger problems.

If any of these are uncovered in the process, expect the price and terms to be revised.

If you find yourself in this position, you must look to your own exit time frame, your state of mind, the stage of your business and the market. Then you must weigh the facts and make an objective decision. This is where a good advisor really helps out.

Chapter 39.

The Biggest Deal Killer

That would be time.

Time can work against you as an entrepreneur or help you depending on what position you are in. But remember, while the buyer is buying your business, you still have existing customers, suppliers, employees and all kinds of moving parts in your business. Your business is still operating. You have to manage your business while you're negotiating to sell it.

For example, the buyer might request financials that you don't have because your bookkeeper has not closed the books.

Or you request that information from your accountant and he's in the middle of tax season. He (and the information) is unavailable for six weeks. This cycle could go on for every due diligence request the buyer makes. When the turnaround time ought to be less than a week, it may take several weeks. This could easily stretch on for months.

Understandably, this creates transaction fatigue for the entrepreneur as well as the buyer. How long can you run a marathon? At some point you are going to get tired. Time becomes a big Achilles heel.

Buyers often develop remorse while waiting weeks on end for due diligence requests. They are likely deploying tremendous financial resources and, especially in this case, time is money.

Also, as time goes on it's entirely possible that your business's revenues decline. Often entrepreneurs mentally check out due to due diligence related distractions. Some have self-imposed mandates of privacy because they don't want any of their key employees to know they are selling. This can create a tremendous amount of extra work and stress on the entrepreneur.

All this can lead to a loss of sales momentum, which can make the buyer walk away or renegotiate a lower price. Keep in mind, the more time stretches out, the more likely market conditions are to change, and during that time, your business could suffer a loss of a key customer, supplier or employee.

On the other hand, sometimes having the due diligence process stretch out may benefit you positively because market conditions could change in your favor, your revenues could start increasing or you might land a big contract.

Many times the entrepreneur is emotionally spent because of the rigors of the due diligence process. It takes the right mindset to successfully navigate this tedious and time-consuming process. This can impact the exit negatively in two ways:

1. The entrepreneur may simply decide to not sell the business after having spent money, time, focus and resources in the selling process.

2. The entrepreneur gets more and more invested in the idea of selling as he or she moves through various hurdles of due diligence. They mentally check out and don't want to stick around, often accommodating and accepting adverse price revisions.

Remember that time is the ultimate killer of transactions.

Turnaround time is essential for reducing due diligence costs as well as ensuring that the transaction will close on a timely basis. The more time that elapses between requests, the greater the chance for seller and/or buyer remorse.

If you think you know how long it will take to sell your company, that's fine. Just heed my advice and add a few months to your number.

Also, while you are knee deep in due diligence, don't lose sight of the necessity of continuing to run the business effectively. The longer the due diligence process takes, the more you need to focus on the fact that sales still need to be made, inventories and receivables managed, employees trained and bills paid. Losing sight of this can derail your exit or lower the previously agreed upon purchase price.

Chapter 40.

Purchase Price Adjustments

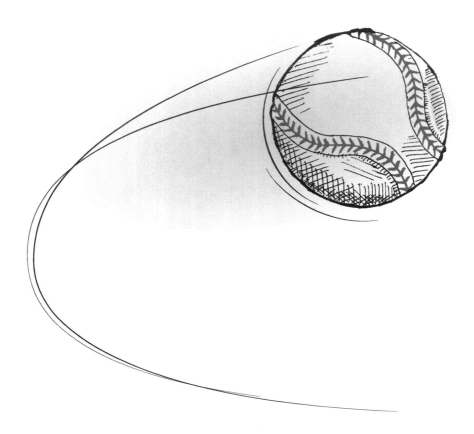

I've said this before; but it's so important, I'm saying it again:

Whatever purchase price you agree to with the buyer, there's a strong likelihood that you really won't collect that purchase price in full.

That's purchase price adjustments, my friend.

You and the buyer agree on a purchase price. The buyer conducts due diligence and finds things that make her figure she's due an adjustment in the purchase price.

The adjustments could be for facility and equipment normalization. This happens when there is a lot of deferred maintenance on your old and outdated equipment or you haven't maintained your facility. The buyer sees that she will have to invest money out of pocket and wants to adjust the purchase price.

Purchase price adjustments could result from any number of things. Product liability claims through date of closing, for example.

Is that even on your radar? Are we even supposed to think like that? How about losses from excluded liabilities? What does that mean? If they're excluded liabilities how can there be losses to the buyer?

I'm here to tell you that there can be any number of scenarios. Other adjustments could be your lease renewal at a higher amount or pension benefit obligation adjustments. It could be contingent adjustments to the purchase price. It could be from failing to get some regulatory approval or clearance for a product. There may be adjustments for off balance sheet liabilities or undisclosed liabilities or under-reserved liabilities. Adjustments can result from any of a thousand and one things.

Chances are, you will see many of these unexpected curve balls thrown at you – and every one means the purchase price gets adjusted downward.

Still standing?

Wait, we haven't talked about the mother of all purchase price adjustments, the ultimate entrepreneur foe: Working capital adjustments.

Working capital adjustments can have a lot of different traps and I'm going to take you through a few real eye poppers.

Even though middle-market companies ($5 million–$1 billion in revenue) are generally bought and sold on a cash-free, debt-free basis, that does not mean working capital. Meaning that while they are buying your company on a cash-free, debt-free basis, they still want your working capital. Most letters of intent refer to cash-free and debt-free businesses. This is SO DECEIVING.

As entrepreneurs, our cash includes our receivables and inventory. What is the difference between that and other cash? You can collect on your receivables and spend that on a nice family vacation just as well as you can with any other cash. Your cash is also easily sucked up in inventory.

This is where the reality check really hurts.

I have come up with some ways to make that a little easier to understand.

Let's split cash into buyer's cash and seller's cash:

Seller's Cash = Excess cash above and beyond reasonable working capital

Buyer's Cash = Reasonable working capital (i.e. receivables, inventory, payables and accruals)

When it comes to buyer's cash (working capital), the entrepreneur may experience several explosions – often after a binding agreement has been signed and the closing has already happened.

Most likely, an escrow amount had been created and a certain percentage of the purchase price was held back and put into this account for a defined period in case of adjustments.

As a part of the negotiation of the purchase and sale agreement, you and the buyer would agree to a working capital hurdle. The working capital hurdle is the target working capital amount you must leave in the business for the business to continue to operate normally.

The working capital hurdle is generally designed to protect the buyer and in some cases could protect the seller as well. The primary purpose of working capital adjustments, however, is to protect the buyer from any games the seller may try to play.

Sellers can, in certain instances, change the make-up of the assets and liabilities of the company without changing the EBITDA. Sellers can play games by slowly paying payables, exponentially speeding up receivables, slowing down new inventory purchases, liquidating existing inventory and reducing work in process.

In many cases, working capital adjustments are gifts from the entrepreneur to the buyer.

Inventory

Let's say you keep quite a bit of excess inventory in your business. Besides the fact that you have sucked up cash building the inventory, it is unlikely that you will be able to sell that excess inventory separately and it will end up being included as normal working capital. Buyers will likely claim that the amount of inventory on hand is the normal amount kept in the business.

If you end up in this position, you have likely subsidized

a fair chunk of your purchase price simply by operating your business in a non-optimal fashion. (Traditionally, the inventory is sold separately for smaller businesses, whereas for many lower middle market and most middle-market companies, inventory is included in the sale price.)

Inventory issues can manifest in other ways as well.

Imagine sitting on a beach somewhere after closing and getting a call from your buyer, who says that 30% of your inventory is obsolete and cannot be repurposed . . . and the dollar amount is a half-million dollars . . . and he is reducing the purchase price . . . and making a claim against the escrow account for that half-million. Nice, huh?

Payables

Don't forget that the buyers are not going to take all your payables. They will likely assume trade payables that are relevant to operating the business. However, many entrepreneurs have payables that are not directly related to the business being sold.

Remember: Operating liabilities benefit the buyer; non-operating liabilities generally benefit the entrepreneur – and these most likely will not get assumed.

So, part of the shocker comes in when you are left holding the bag on a chunk of these excluded payables that you now have to service from your sales proceeds.

Accounts Receivable

Let's say you and the buyer have agreed that you will leave three million dollars' worth of working capital in the business. In most businesses, the biggest chunk of that working capital is receivables. Let's assume you've got two million dollars' worth of receivables outstanding and, like most companies, these receivables are a combination of 30-, 60- and 90-day receivables.

In the buyer's eyes, there is a risk of collection associated with those receivables. To counter the risk of collection, the buyer can take many different paths. One likely approach is that he or she will give you 90% credit for the 30-day receivables, 75% credit for the 60-day receivables and 50% credit for the 90-day receivables.

In the example shown in the table, your $2 million in receivables would get a discount of $370,000. You are $370,000 short in working capital and this working capital shortfall will come in the form of a working capital adjustment.

Receivable	Original Amount	Discount	Discount Amount	Revised Amount
30 days	1,200,000	10%	$120,000	$1,080,000
60 days	600,000	25%	$150,000	$450,000
90 days	200,000	50%	$100,000	$100,000
Total	$2,000,000		$370,000	$1,630,000

Working Capital Shortage

In simple terms, the purchase price will go down and the money that was held back, or payable in the future, will do likewise.

But wait . . . it gets worse. The buyer will also likely enforce a time limit during which he or she will apply these receivables to the calculation of the working capital. When all is said and done, it's entirely possible that the buyer will not have to give you any credit for the receivables collected beyond 90 days.

Say you have a $500,000 receivable that you have been fighting to bring in and on the 95th day post-closing that $500k receivable comes in. Friend, you will likely get zero credit for that.

Working capital adjustments can manifest in other ways as well. Perhaps you are selling your company mid-year and post-closing, when your balance sheet is reconciled, the buyer calls to say that, because you have not been accruing bonuses, sick pay and vacations, he has to make a $200,000 adjustment. This means $200,000 less in your pocket. Otherwise, he has to take it out of his pocket – and no buyer is going to want to do that.

If you're not operating your business optimally, not only can this reduce your selling price, it can potentially subsidize the purchase price for the benefit of the buyer.

And that's not what you had in mind when you decided to sell your business.

Chapter 41.

Third Parties

You figured it was going to be between just you and the buyer, right?

Wrong.

Now you've got to worry about third parties.

These third parties play a huge role in whether the transaction will get done or not.

Why? When a company is sold, there are typically a host of third-party clearances and/or approvals needed and if the third party has an issue, that can easily challenge or delay the transaction.

Third parties could be landlords, lenders and lessors, key suppliers, investors, unions or environmental, government or regulatory agencies, etc. We often read about anti-trust issues in newspapers. This is a classic form of third-party clearance for companies of a certain size and market position.

Many times, exits are derailed by a lawsuit or the threat of a lawsuit that popped up out of nowhere. Depending on the size of the issue, the exit transaction can fall apart. In some cases, the issue is related to disputes with customers or suppliers, which could have material repercussions on the future of the business.

In many cases, they are product-warranty claims related to products sold and being used by customers.

In the case of lawsuits, the size and implications matter greatly. If there is a $25,000 lawsuit in a $30 million acquisition, it likely will not be a big issue. However, sometimes even small lawsuits or claims can derail an exit. For example, minor product-warranty claims that signal a red flag for large amounts of potential claims in the future.

Bottom line: Be aware of the role third parties play in the sale of your business. To avoid unnecessary delays, it is imperative for the entrepreneur to review leases and contemplate other third-party issues in advance of putting the company up for sale. Create a competent advisory team and proactively deal with issues that could serve as obstacles.

Chapter 42.

Legal Exposures

When entrepreneurs sell their businesses, or even consider selling their businesses, they seldom think of legal liability. Most would say, "Legal liability for what?"

You may be surprised to know that there are multitudes of legal liabilities that can come back and haunt you. Many entrepreneurs play games only to end up with major nosebleeds later on. Conversely, many shrewd buyers prey on unprepared sellers and their advisors.

Let's start with the basics. You may know the term "representations and warranties" (also called reps and warranties), but you may not be entirely clear about what reps and warranties are and why they should matter to you.

Representations = **Statements** made by the entrepreneur

Warranties = **Promises** given by the entrepreneur

What the seller wants is for the entrepreneur to make all-encompassing statements and loads of promises about the business. The more all-encompassing your statements (representations) and promises (warranties), the more you will get screwed later. Your attorney may refer to this as "the buyer wanting broad language around representations and warranties."

Why does the buyer want these statements and promises from the entrepreneur? Simply put, the buyer is using these statements and promises to justify valuation and/or determine the value for your business. You will be required to give representations around all kinds of things, from accuracy of financial information to customers and supplier agreements to different types of contracts and intellectual property.

And if you have misrepresented or not disclosed a material fact, this can create potential claims against the escrow account and other deferred and contingent payments or outright claims directly against you.

The buyer wants some safeguards against representations (statements) and warranties (promises) from you for undisclosed liabilities, under-reserved liabilities or outright misrepresentations.

If you don't have decent representation, you could get yourself in a whole lot of trouble really fast.

As I've said, the world of selling your business is very unfair, most often geared to protect the buyer and almost never the seller.

Therefore, be clear and accurate when you make statements to a potential buyer. Don't over-promise – while it is okay to be positive about your company's strengths and opportunities, temper your remarks so they don't come back to haunt you.

As referenced in the next graphic, the buyer has all kinds of methods and safeguards to reduce the purchase price or collect monies directly paid to you.

Beware:
Buying Process Skewed Against the Entrepreneur

STEP ①

Buyer Identifies & Verifies Assets, Liabilities, Operations Risks & Opportunities

STEP ②

Buyer May Reduce Purchase Price by Finding All Kinds of Things in Due Diligence

STEP ③

Buyer Gets Statements & Promises From Entrepreneur (aka Representations & Warranties)

STEP ④

ESCALATE

ESCALATE

Buyer Can Lower Purchase Price Further by Using Adjustments After the Closing for Working Capital, Taxes, Hidden Liabilities, Off Balance Sheet Liabilities etc.

Buyer Has Financial Mechanisms to Collect by Making Claims Against Holdbacks/ Escrows, etc.

Buyer Has Legal Recourse to Protect Their Interest Using Set-Off Rights, Sandbagging Claims, Clawbacks, Dispute Resolution, Litigation etc.

Sandbagging Claims

We entrepreneurs sign an initial letter of intent and then open our books to let the buyer put us through intense, months-long scrutiny, looking into every nook and cranny of our businesses, and it's entirely possible for the buyer to become aware of certain deficiencies that even we don't know about.

Let's say that the buyer finds out that you are not in compliance with the law in some element of how you operate your business. Knowing this, he or she can go ahead and close the transaction, buy the business and then come after you for recourse against that issue. That, my friend, is called sandbagging.

This is where the entrepreneur needs a specialist attorney to create a good anti-sandbagging provision that essentially states that the buyer has been provided all information and has been able to conduct due diligence of the company and under no circumstance will the entrepreneur have any liability for any breach of any covenant, representation or warranty to the extent that the buyer knew of such breach as of the closing date. (I know that's a lot of legal language, but not having this kind of clause can open you up for unnecessary hurt.)

Set-Off Rights

Buyers almost always want to shift risk to the entrepreneur. It is important for the entrepreneur to understand that the buyer usually has an upper hand to begin with, simply because of the way the sale is structured. For example, a portion of the sale may be held back and a portion may be in the form of contingent or deferred payments.

If something occurs that the buyer feels is a breach of a representation, covenant or warranty, that's where set-off rights come in. These rights give the buyer the right to withhold funds that are already in his possession. Now, this is different from an escrow agreement, which is generally governed by an agreement wherein the funds are typically held at a third-party financial institution, and the buyer would make a claim against those funds.

Set-off rights are much more advantageous to the buyer because he already has the funds. The only possible recourse left in that type of scenario is, most likely, litigation.

Buyers will use these set-off rights as a very effective way to ensure that the seller does what he is supposed to do. Buyers can adjust future, deferred or contingent payments against their claim by using these set-off rights.

Cross-Default Provisions

These can be another nasty surprise for the entrepreneur. Many times when a business is sold, additional agreements are added. Perhaps your company has multiple divisions and the buyer is only buying one of them. However, the buyer wants the parent company to provide services or some form of technology to the entity being purchased.

Cross-default provisions come into play if the entrepreneur is not compliant with post-closing conditions. In the case of non-competition, for example, the buyer triggers the cross-default provisions and could cancel all contracts with the entrepreneur. Once these cross-default provisions are invoked, the entrepreneur is not likely to have much recourse against the buyer.

Indemnification

Most purchase and sale agreements are going to have

some kind of dispute resolution language that essentially requires binding or mandatory arbitration. While the buyer will initially make claims against holdback escrows, deferred payments and contingent payments, they can also claw back a portion of the purchase price. You could also be in a position where the buyer could come after you for above and beyond what he has already paid you.

This is particularly applicable in situations where you and your advisors have not negotiated adequate indemnification caps on your liability.

Let's say that the buyer uses your technology in her supply chain, incorporating your technology into her products. They subsequently sell two million units. Quickly, a barrage of product warranty claims start coming in because of some flaw in your technology. The company has to do a massive recall. The buyer relied on your representations and warranties and she wants blood.

If you don't have adequate indemnification, you have a real problem.

On the other hand, you may have a buyer who wants to make claims against you for the smallest of things. In this situation, it is wise to negotiate a threshold or deductible amount, so you can avoid dealing with minor claims. (When using a "threshold," the buyer must wait to make a claim until he or she has losses at least equal to or more than the agreed upon threshold amount. Once the threshold amount is reached, the buyer is then paid for all losses — back to the first dollar. When using a "deductible," the buyer must absorb the first "X amount of dollars" and is paid only on losses in excess of the deductible amount.)

In many cases, sellers and their advisors fail to negotiate indemnification differently for minority stockholders. For example: If your sister owns 5% of your company, do you really want her to have joint and several liability along with you – especially if you have not negotiated a proper indemnification cap – subjecting her to significant financial risk?

In a joint and several liability scenario, the buyer can come after not just you but all parties involved including, in this example, your sister, who was a minority shareholder. It's up to the defendants to figure out their particular portions of liability and payment. Essentially, if the buyer doesn't collect from you, they will collect from your sister or other shareholders.

My message to you is that you are not in the clear simply because you have collected your money in the sale.

You may have trailing legal liabilities that can come and bite you after you have sold the business. This is where you need to sit down with a competent M&A attorney to understand the potential legal risks as well as the possible financial consequences and how to best limit them.

Conclusion

Exit Bomb. Why Most Entrepreneurs Can't Sell, Don't Sell or Sell Their Company For Peanuts.

One Last Thing . . . Or Four

Have I talked you out of selling your business? Have I convinced you to stay with your company until they take you out feet first?

I hope not. That wasn't my purpose in writing this book.

What I do want is to help you make sure you're not taken to the cleaners when you sell.

In other words, I want to help you make certain that the Exit Bomb doesn't blow up your future plans in a ten-block radius.

I've covered a lot of ground here, but I want to leave you with a few last pieces of advice:

1. Start Now

Even if business is booming and selling is the last thing

on your mind, start planning for your exit now. If you've already planned to sell your business, my advice is to delay it – if at all possible – to get everything in order. If you can't wait, you have to expect to take a hit on the selling price if you don't have time for a comprehensive cleanup.

Visit www.ExitBomb.Org/Programs and create an Exit Program to help you clean up, enhance value and subsequently exit your company for maximum value. Programs are available for external exits (third-party sale), internal transitions (transfer to family or sale to employees) and even "No Exit Exits" (maintain ownership with no active involvement). Programs are tailored to your exit timeline and can range from a few months to a few years.

2. Get Yourself Ready

Here's a checklist of some of the things you'll need to do to get yourself ready for your exit with the biggest payday possible:

- [ ] Start Many Years Prior (If Possible)
- [ ] Set Goals
- [ ] Identify Timeline
- [ ] Create a Team
- [ ] Review Personal & Family Considerations
- [ ] Identify Valuation Range
- [ ] Identify Exit Options
- [ ] Be Clear on Life After Business
- [ ] Align Stakeholders
- [ ] Conduct Net Proceeds Analysis
- [ ] Identify & Optimize Tax Impact
- [ ] Review Assets Outside Business
- [ ] Review Impact of Lost Perks
- [ ] Review Impact of Potential Exclusions
- [ ] Calculate Liabilities & Exposures
- [ ] Conduct Retirement Shortfall Analysis
- [ ] Be Clear About Post-Transaction Involvement
- [ ] Understand Destructive Exit Motivations
- [ ] Get into an Asset-Oriented Mindset
- [ ] Avoid Being Emotional
- [ ] Keep it Confidential

3. Get Your Business Ready

Below is just a sampling of things that need to happen to your company if you expect to not leave a chunk of your life's work on the table.

- ☐ Understand Your Value Drivers
- ☐ Understand Your Risk Drivers
- ☐ Understand Your Vulnerabilities
- ☐ Improve Financial Transparency
- ☐ Cut Costs/Improve Margins
- ☐ Optimize Taxes
- ☐ Create Recurring Revenue
- ☐ Diversify Revenues
- ☐ Diversify Products
- ☐ Diversify Suppliers
- ☐ Diversify Customers
- ☐ Diversify Industry
- ☐ Build Barriers to Entry
- ☐ Build Competitive Differentiators
- ☐ Protect Intellectual Property
- ☐ Build Depth/Breadth in Management Team
- ☐ Get Employee Contracts
- ☐ Build Golden Handcuffs for Key Employees
- ☐ Get Non-Performers Off the Ship
- ☐ Document Systems & Processes
- ☐ Update & Maintain Facilities & Equipment
- ☐ Collect & Organize All Company Data & Supporting Materials
- ☐ Align Stakeholders on Valuation/Timing
- ☐ Lay Out Plan to Select, Groom & Integrate Successor
- ☐ Onboard Your replacement
- ☐ Fire Yourself at Your Earliest Convenience

Do that and you've likely defused that damned Exit Bomb.

4. What Next?

Whether you intend to exit in the near future or ten years from now, you need to start preparing. And the way to do that is by figuring out where you stand now.

We make that easy with a complimentary **Exit Bomb Readiness Score.**™ Just answer a few questions online and we'll share a report with you that provides an Exit Score to help you determine how prepared you are. Once you know, you'll be well on your way to setting up a game plan for your next steps.

To get your complimentary Exit Bomb Readiness Score™ visit www.ExitBomb.Org/Score.

You are Not Alone

Thinking about exiting your business can be pretty scary. But it isn't something you have to face alone.

We've built an organization to help you clean up, enhance value and subsequently exit your company on your own terms and timeline ... and for maximum value. It's the Exit Bomb Organization™. Created by entrepreneurs for entrepreneurs, the Exit Bomb Organization is a privately-held organization which offers a variety of tools and programs to help entrepreneurs and the independent advisors who work with them:

Exit Bomb Readiness Score™: A high-level assessment to help you gauge your current state of exit readiness relative to Exit Bomb Organization benchmarks.

Exit Bomb Readiness Analysis™: A comprehensive exercise to help the entrepreneur and their management understand key variables, components, risks, obstacles and opportunities that can increase or decrease business value. A detailed report that highlights issues in the company that need to be addressed prior to exit.

Exit Maximization Programs™: We leverage our proprietary tools and intellectual property to create custom exit maximization programs that help you accomplish your goals and subsequently exit for maximum value. Programs are available for external exits (third-party sale), internal transitions (transfer to family or sale to employees) and even "No Exit Exits" (maintain ownership with no active involvement.) Programs are tailored to your exit timeline and can range from a few months to a few years. All are guided by Exit Bomb advisors.

Exit Bomb Network™: A band of carefully selected advisors trained to administer and implement Exit Bomb Programs. There's also a deep network of potential buyers for your business. All to help you improve the odds of leaving your company without leaving money on the table.

Exit Bomb Workshops™: Workshops that explore the key elements of the Exit Bomb and the techniques needed to defuse it. The Workshops drive home the key steps entrepreneurs must take to clean up and optimize their companies in order to avoid business wealth destruction.

Visit www.ExitBomb.Org to learn more.

Who the Heck Is Gower Idrees and Why Should You Care?

No special reason – unless you want to avoid leaving money on the table when you exit your business. Gower Idrees has spent a lifetime researching why most entrepreneurs do precisely that. His specialized knowledge can help you clean up, enhance value and subsequently exit your company for the maximum payout. But Gower doesn't offer mere theory; he speaks from hard-won personal experience, having built and exited several companies successfully. The founder of the Exit Bomb Organization and CEO of Oregon-based M&A firm RareBrain, Gower has advised some of America's fastest growing companies. His many media appearances include The Wall Street Journal, Bloomberg Television, SUCCESS magazine and Yahoo Finance. Gower spent over a decade in the Entrepreneur Organization (EO) and is the past president of EO-Houston.

For representation inquiries and speaking engagements, Please visit www.RareBrain.com/Contact

Twitter: @GowerIdrees

Bibliography

Andriole, S. J. (2009). *Technology Due Diligence: Best Practices for Chief Information Officers, Venture Capitalists, and Technology Vendors.* Hershey, PA: Information Science Reference.

Cook, R. (2011). *Selling Your Technology Company for Maximum Value: A comprehensive guide for entrepreneurs.* Petersfield, Hampshire, Great Britain: Harriman House.

Feld, B., & Mendelson, J. (2013). *Venture Deals: Be Smarter Than Your Lawyer and Venture Capitalist.* Hoboken, NJ: John Wiley & Sons, Inc.

Filippell, M. A. (2011). *Mergers and Acquisitions Playbook: Lessons from the Middle-Market Trenches.* Hoboken, NJ: John Wiley & Sons, Inc.

Gabriel, C. (1998). *How to Sell Your Business - And Get What You Want!: A Pragmatic Guide With Revealing Tips from 57 Sellers.* Westport, CT: Gwent Press Inc.

Glazier, S. C. (2004). *Technology Deals, Case Studies for Officers, Directors, Investors, and General Counsels about IPO's, Mergers, Acquisitions, Venture Capital, ... Due Diligence and Patent Strategies.* Washington, D.C.: LBI Law and Business Institute

Hams, B. (2012). *Ownership Thinking: How to End Entitlement and Create a Culture of Accountability, Purpose, and Profit.* New York, NY: McGraw-Hill.

Harper, S. C. (2013). *Here's to the Crazy Entrepreneurs: Is Entrepreneurism a Mental Disorder?* North Charleston, SC: CreateSpace.

Homan, T., & Meyer, D. (2013). *Beat the Exit Bubble: The Ultimate Guide for Exiting Your Business.* Denver, CO: Execute on Strategy LLC.

Hooke, J. C. (1995). *M&A: A Practical Guide to Doing the Deal.* Hoboken, NJ: John Wiley & Sons, Inc.

Jackim, R. E., & Christman, P. G. (2006). *The $10 Trillion Opportunity: Designing Successful Exit Strategies for Middle Market Business Owners, Second Edition* (2nd Edition ed.). Palatine, IL: Exit Planning Institute.

Kaplan, S. (2009). *Sell Your Business for the Max!* New York, NY: Workman Publishing Company, Inc.

Lajoux, A. R., & Elson, C. M. (2000). *The Art of M&A Due Diligence.* New York, NY: McGraw-Hill.

Marks, K. H., Robbins, L. E., Fernandez, G., Funkhouser, J. P., & Williams, D. (2009). *The Handbook of Financing Growth: Strategies, Capital Structure, and M&A Transactions.* Hoboken, NJ: John Wiley & Sons, Inc.

Marks, K. H., Slee, R. T., Blees, C. W., & Nall, M. R. (2012). *Middle Market M & A: Handbook for Investment Banking and Business Consulting.* Hoboken, NJ: John Wiley & Sons, Inc.

Mellen, C. M., & Evans, F. C. (2010). *Valuation for M&A: Building Value in Private Companies.* Hoboken, NJ: John Wiley & Sons, Inc.

Miller, W. D. (2010). *Value Maps: Valuation Tools That Unlock Business Wealth (1st Edition ed.).* Hoboken, NJ: John Wiley & Sons, Inc.

Oakley, J. T. (2012). *You Sold Your Company - Envisioning the Changes.* Corpus Christi, TX: Keysar Publishing Company.

Paulson, E., & Huber, C. (2001). *The Technology M&A Guidebook.* Hoboken, NJ: John Wiley & Sons, Inc.

Slee, R. T. (2011). *Private Capital Markets: Valuation, Capitalization, and Transfer of Private Business Interests + Website* (2nd Edition ed.). Hoboken, NJ: John Wiley & Sons, Inc.

Stieglitz, R. G., & Sorkin, S. H. (2010). *Expensive Mistakes When Buying & Selling Companies ... And How To Avoid Them In Your Deals.* Potomac, MD: Acuity Publishing.

Vanwyck, W. (2010). *The Business Transition Crisis: Plan Your Succession Now to Beat the Biggest Business Selloff in History.* New York, NY: BPS Books.

West, T. (2013). *2013 Business Reference Guide: The Essential Guide to Pricing Businesses and Franchises* (23rd Edition ed.). Anaheim, CA: Business Brokerage Press.

Glossary of Terms and Phrases

Acquisition Strategy (Horizontal) – An acquisition plan in which the purchasing company is focused on expanding its own operations by buying external companies whose products or services are very similar to the purchaser's own products and services. This is typically done in an attempt to expand the purchaser's market share and/or consolidate distribution and/or retailer channels.

Acquisition Strategy (Vertical) – An acquisition plan in which a purchasing company attempts to purchase external companies whose operations are complementary to the purchaser within a specific industry. This is typically done in an attempt to reduce reliance on outside suppliers, better control the combined companies' operating costs or create a new barrier to entry for competitors.

Adjacency Strategy – An acquisition strategy that has the primary purpose of adding products or services that are very similar or complementary to a company's current products or services.

Arbitrage (Valuation Multiple) – A purchasing company's use of its publicly-traded shares, which are trading at a price that is a given multiple of one or more important valuation metrics (e.g. revenues, earnings), to pay for the purchase of another company at a private valuation that reflects a lower multiple of the same valuation metric(s) for the purchased company.

Asset-Light Company – A company with relatively few tangible assets and/or minimal capital expenditure requirements.

Asset (Off Balance Sheet) – Any asset whose market value is significantly different (typically higher) than the value reflected on a company's balance sheet.

Asset Normalization – An adjustment process that identifies the current market or other value of an asset compared to the value currently claimed on a company's balance sheet.

Barrier to Entry – Any factor that makes it difficult for new competitors to enter an existing market for specific products or services.

Baseline Valuation – Informal initial "As Is" estimate of a company's "value," established with the intention of subsequently taking certain actions that will increase that value significantly.

Benchmarking – Establishing average performance or other measurable standards among similar companies in order to establish a "yardstick" with which to measure a specific company's performance.

Capital Expenditures (CAPEX) – Expenses related to, or investments in tangible assets typically subject to, multiple years of depreciation (with the exception of real estate).

Capital Expenditures (Expenses) – Expenses related to tangible assets but whose recurring or temporary nature allows them to be accounted for as expenses in the year they are incurred.

Capitalization – The sum of a company's long-term debt, retained earnings and all other elements of the owner's equity.

Carryover Liability – A debt or other obligation that will continue to be the responsibility of a company's current owner after the sales transaction is completed.

Cash Conversion Cycle (CCC) – A cash flow calculation that measures the time a business takes to convert its investment in inventory and other resources into cash. In simple words, it is a measure of how long cash is tied up in certain business assets before something can be sold and cash collected from the customer.

Clawback – A provision in a sales agreement that allows the buyer to reduce an asset owned by the seller (e.g. cash held in escrow) by an agreed upon amount after the sale is completed given that certain events do (or do not) occur within a specific time frame.

Comps – Short for "comparables." Any collection of measures of company valuation (e.g. share prices as multiples of earnings) or operational efficiency (e.g. gross or net profit margins) across a group of similar companies.

Comingle – Use of corporate funds to pay personal expenses, or vice versa, creating potential tax savings for a company owner, but clouding the company's true operating costs for both the owner and any potential buyer.

Consideration – The total amount of money and other valuable items (e.g. shares in the buyer's company) that is offered as payment in the sale. May include many short-term and longer-term components.

Consolidation – The reduction of the number of companies active in a particular market as a result of a series of acquisitions of small competitors by one or a few large competitors.

Contingent Adjustment – Any post-closing change in

total consideration paid in the sale of a company based on the achievement or non-achievement of a specific financial goal (e.g. revenue or earnings growth) or other event after the close.

Contingent Payment – Any additional payment due from the buyer to the seller post-closing based on the achievement or non-achievement of a specific financial goal or other event after the closing has occurred.

Cross-Default Provision – Any provision in a sales contract that creates a liability for a third party when one party to the contract does not perform as agreed upon in the contract.

Cyclicality – A measure of the degree to which a particular company or industry's growth and profitability reflect a consistent link with the economic cycle.

Depreciation Recapture – A tax code requirement that declares accelerated depreciation on a tangible asset must be reversed and the amount of the reversal taxed at the owner's ordinary (maximum) tax rate.

Due Diligence – A potential buyer's detailed investigation of a target company's assets, liabilities, financials, customer and supplier relationships and all other elements of potential value or liability.

Due Diligence (Reverse) – A pro-active exercise carried out in advance by a company's owner to prepare and confirm all information a potential buyer will potentially require in order to fully understand and value the company.

Earn-Out – A provision in a sales contract that requires a specific event to occur (e.g. a minimum level of post-closing revenue or earnings growth) within a particular amount of time in order for a specific amount of post-closing consideration to actually be paid to the seller.

EBITDA – Short for "Earnings Before Interest, Taxes, Depreciation and Amortization." In merger & acquisition transactions, EBITDA is a commonly used by corporate finance professionals to determine a company's potential value based on known valuations of similar companies in the same industry.

Exclusions – Corporate assets and liabilities that the buyer of a company does not assume as part of the sale transaction.

Exclusivity – Seller's agreement to not have discussions with other potential buyers of the company within a specific time frame, allowing a single buyer to complete his or her due diligence and negotiations with the seller without interference from any other buyer.

Exit Channel – Any potential means of discontinuing the ownership of a business, ranging from liquidating the company to selling it to employees, family members or an unrelated buyer.

Exit Value – The total consideration realized by the seller of a company, which varies depending on the exit channel chosen.

Financial Engineering – Use of sophisticated or complicated accounting or financial strategies by financial experts to create or reveal hidden value or cash flow in an asset that is otherwise not easily identifiable by other parties.

Free Cash Flow (FCF) – The amount of cash a company gains or loses as a result of its operations during a given period after all expenses and capital expenditures are taken into account.

Indemnification Cap – M&A transactions involving privately-held companies generally include "indemnification" provisions requiring the seller's stockholders to pay the buyer for certain losses and liabilities that they incur in connection with the purchase of the underlying company. Sellers can negotiate to have a cap on their liability to minimize risk.

Intellectual Property (IP) – Intangible assets created by the application of a company's employees' or owners' intellectual effort, knowledge or experience (e.g. patents, trade secrets, copyrights).

Letter of Intent (LOI) – Generally, a non-binding agreement between buyer and seller that typically includes an initial price, key terms, proposed structure and allocation of risk. Once signed by both parties, an LOI typically marks the starting point for buyer's due diligence to begin.

Leverage – The ratio of a company's level of debt compared to its owner's equity and retained earnings.

Lifestyle Expenses – An owner's personal expenses that are paid by the company with its cash.

Liquidity – A measure of the ease and speed with which an asset can be converted into cash. May also refer to the amount of cash or near-cash assets (such as certificates of deposit) a company has available.

Margins – Short for "profit margins," which can include gross margin (revenues minus cost of goods) or net margin (net after-tax earnings as a percentage of total revenue).

Multiple – In the case of company valuations, the ratio of the offering price for the company divided by a particular financial measure (such as total assets, revenue,

EBITDA or net income). Often used by corporate finance professionals to determine a company's potential value based on known valuations of similar companies in the same industry.

Net Proceeds – The final amount a company's seller receives from the buyer, excluding all fees, commissions, taxes and other deductions and costs incurred in order to complete the sale transaction.

Obsolescence – The state in which a product or service is no longer desired due to the availability of an alternative replacement that has more advantages and conveniences as compared to the original product or service.

Purchase and Sale Agreement – The legal document containing all elements of the final agreement between buyer and seller, including all terms, conditions, covenants and provisions related to each party's responsibilities and obligations to be fulfilled subsequent to the closing date.

Purchase Price Adjustment – A provision in a purchase and sale contract that provides for a specific change in the agreed purchase price based on a specified action or event occurring or not occurring before or after the transaction close date.

Recapitalization – A restructuring of the mix of a company's current long-term debt and/or owner's equity, typically achieved by adding new debt or equity.

Return on Investment (ROI) – Calculation of all cash flows (e.g. interest payments, resale value) an investor receives from a particular investment, typically expressed as an average annual percentage.

Roll-Up – See **Consolidation** (above)

Sandbagging – A clause giving the buyer the right to

make a claim after closing for material information that a buyer knew was incorrect (and knowingly did not inform the seller) prior to closing.

Seasonality – A measure of the degree to which a particular company's or industry's growth and profitability reflect a consistent link with recurring annual events and circumstances such as weather, holidays, school schedules, sports seasons etc.

Seller Financing – Any portion of consideration to the seller that involves the seller agreeing to be paid according to a pre-agreed periodic (usually monthly or quarterly) payment schedule.

Set-Off Right – The buyer's contractual post-closing right to reduce an amount owed to the seller by the same amount as a liability or expense not known at the time of closing.

Sinking Fund – A planned series of cash deposits set up to provide a target final amount available for a specific purpose, such as buying an expensive asset or creating a pool of funds from which certain incentive payments can be made at a later date.

Stakeholders – Every person or party with an economic interest in the success of a company or its sale, including shareholders, family members and employees. In some cases this can include a company's suppliers and customers.

Synergized Value – An increased value resulting from combining the selling company with the buying company, which is greater than the sum of the value of the two companies separately.

Synergy – The economic or financial equivalent of 1 + 1 =

3, reflecting additional financial returns without the addition of new assets or expenses. While synergies can vary, some synergy is typically available in an acquisition due to the removal of redundant expenses.

Valuation – A value put on a company using a host of different calculating methods, the result of which may or may not reflect the price the company's owner would actually receive from selling the company.

Valuation Gap – The difference between different parties' estimates of value for a company. Typically, this term refers to the difference between the price a seller expects to receive for his company and the price a buyer is actually willing to pay.

Vet – Checking the facts and figures provided by another party.

Working Capital – Current assets minus current liabilities, generally considered to be a measure of a company's ability to fund growth from internal cash flows rather than requiring additional long-term debt or equity.

Working Capital Adjustment – Adjustments made to various working capital accounts (e.g. inventory, accounts receivable, accounts payable) to ensure that the company being bought will have the required level of working capital needed to continue normal operations post-acquisition.

Made in the USA
San Bernardino, CA
19 November 2015